Chinese 1000

中国话一千

Idiomatic and Colloquial Expressions

中国话
习惯用法和口语的表达法

Mandarin Chinese/English

by

Jerome P. Keuper, Ph.D.
杰睿　古柏　博士

Krieger Publishing Company, Malabar, Florida

Original Edition 1997

Printed and Published by
KRIEGER PUBLISHING COMPANY
KRIEGER DRIVE
MALABAR, FLORIDA 32950

Copyright © 1997 by Jerome P. Keuper

Library of Congress Cataloging-In-Publication Data

Keuper, Jerome P., 1921–
    Chinese 1000 : idiomatic and colloquial expressions, Mandarin
    Chinese/English / by Jerome P. Keuper = [Chung-kuo hua i chi' ien :
    Chung-kuo hua hsi kuan yung fa ho k' ou yü ti piao ta fa / Chieh-jui
    Ku-po]
        p.   cm.
    Includes bibliographical references and index.
    ISBN 1-57524-006-8 (hardcover : alk. paper).
    ISBN 1-57524-047-5 (paperback : alk. paper).
    1. Chinese language—Idioms—Dictionaries.   2. Chinese language–
    –Dictionaries—English.   I. Title.
    PL1273.K48   1997
    495.1'321—dc21
                                                            96-50318
                                                            CIP

10   9   8   7   6   5   4   3   2

"tiān bú pà dì bú pà
jìu pà yáng gǔi zi
shūo zhōng gúo hùa"

I don't fear Heaven
I don't fear Hell
I only fear Americans
speaking Chinese!

..... author unknown

Dedication .....

To my wife, Natalie.

Acknowledgements .....

I would like to acknowledge the invaluable help of Tsuo-Hsien Liu with the translations. I thank Wen Sun Simmons and Hsueh Ching Lee for their many suggestions, and my daughter Melanie Johnson for typing the original manuscript.

I am grateful to Professor Junda Lin, Ph.D., at Florida Institute of Technology (F.I.T.) for his thorough review of the manuscript and valuable suggestions. I am also indebted to Dong Zhang at F.I.T. and to the F.I.T. Chinese Students and Scholars Friendship Association for their interest and participation in the project.

Two others at F.I.T. provided considerable assistance in preparing camera-ready manuscripts for review and publication. Eric Li, a Ph.D. candidate, spent many hours at the computer to enter the simplified Chinese characters and pinyin tone marks into files for laser printing. Professor Maurice K. Kurtz, Jr., Ph.D., configured an appropriate computer system with a Chinese character kit, developed computerized tone marks for the pinyin syllables, served as editor, and coordinated publication details.

Dr. Zuyan Zhou provided final proof-reading for which I am duly grateful.

Lastly, I want to thank the late Dr. Arthur Kimball for his interest and constant encouragement in the development of this dictionary.

Jerome P. Keuper, Ph.D.

Contents .....

About the Author .....

In World War II Dr. Keuper served as an intelligence officer in the O.S.S. in the China - Burma - India Theater and was awarded the "China Medal" by the Chinese government. After the war Dr. Keuper entered Massachusetts Institute of Technology (M.I.T.) The Chinese graduate students invited him to live with them in their own apartment building in Cambridge. He had met several of them in the Orient during the war.

Following M.I.T. he pursued graduate studies in physics at Stanford University and the University of Virginia where he received a Ph.D. in nuclear physics. He is also the recipient of five honorary doctorates. As a scientist he contributed to the development of America's space program in the early years at Cape Canaveral, Florida.

In 1958 Dr. Keuper founded Florida Institute of Technology and served an unprecedented 28 years as its first president. Today he is President Emeritus and a Life Member of the Board of Trustees of the University.

Dr. Keuper assumed many leadership positions outside the University. He served two terms as Chairman of the Board of Directors of the Federal Reserve Bank of Atlanta (Jacksonville Branch). He is an avid collector of palms and is past President of The International Palm Society. In recognition of his creation of a botanical garden he was awarded the 1975 "Silver Medal" of the National Council of State Garden Clubs.

He is well known internationally for his work in the restoration of pre-war MG motor cars. He has participated in MG events in Europe, Australia, and South Africa and established a Registry of these rare vehicles in North America.

Dr. Keuper played a prominent role in creating an all volunteer Alliance between the country of Colombia and the state of Florida. Later he served on the international board of Partners of the Americas. He is fluent in Spanish, and Colombia dedicated an elementary school in Bogotá in his name.

He found time to make six visits to R.O.C. and P.R.C. to recruit students and continue his study of the Chinese language. Dr. Keuper encouraged a close relationship between Florida Institute of Technology and Taiwan. He was awarded the "Medal of Highest Honor" of VACRS, the Vocational Assistance Commission for Retired Serviceman, Republic of China.

Recently he was chosen to be East Central Florida's Laureate for induction into the "Junior Achievement Hall of Fame" for 1995.

Foreword .....

One might imagine that to the Chinese there is really nothing idiomatic about their language - it is all "just good
Chinese." To the beginning student of Chinese as a foreign language, however, everything about the language
may initially seem idiomatic. *Chinese 1000* was designed
to be a ready reference to this perplexing world of
idioms and colloquial expressions in Mandarin Chinese
(pǔ tōng huà). While first and second year study students should find it an especially enriching supplement
to their textbooks, anyone with an interest in the
language can benefit from having at hand "just the right
words" to sum up situations in succinct and colorful ways.

Usefulness in everyday speech was a criterion for the
one thousand entries collected here. The scope is broad.
Customary expressions of courtesy are included, usually
in several variants. There are also rude sayings and
expletives - always advantageous to understand, although
the speaker employs them at his or her own risk! Slang
words, whose nonstandard use is unlikely to be explained
in Chinese to English dictionaries, form another cate-
gory in this treasury of colloquial speech.

Most items would be considered true idioms, phrases
whose meanings are not apparent from the sense of the
individual words. For instance, if someone is "adding
oil, adding vinegar" jiā yóu jiā cù　加 油 加 醋, he's
not dressing a salad but "exaggerating." On the other

hand, an absolutely nonsensical sequence of words, "blow cow (skin)" chuī niú (pí) 吹 牛 (皮), indicates the kind of conflated talk that means "to boast or brag." Also among *Chinese 1000's* entries is a response to being praised which, however welcome, and even deserved, becomes hyperbole in our polite declining of the compliment "You overly award me!" guò jiǎng! 过 奖！

Some idioms follow a logic that calls to mind a familiar saying in English. Whenever possible, the author has provided idiomatic equivalents, after giving a word for word translation. By the "turning" of an eye in Chinese, zhuǎn yǎn 转 眼, we have the instantaneous moment of the "twinkling" of an eye in English. The Chinese colloquialism "not donkey, not horse" fēi lǘ fēi mǎ 非 驴 非 马 is aptly rendered "neither fish nor fowl."

Teachers of Chinese will appreciate that so many of the entries in Jerome P. Keuper's selection build upon the basic vocabulary which beginning and intermediate students are typically expected to master. The selection can be used to reinforce and extend the materials presented in class. For example, when the phrase yí lù píng ān 一 路 平 安 comes up as a new term in the textbook, students can easily locate it in *Chinese 1000's* alphabetic arrangement and compare it with other phrases that begin with "yí lù..." for wishing someone a safe or comfortable journey.

There is, of course, the straightforward dǐng hǎo 顶 好 to approve of something "very good," but in addition the more resonantly enthusiastic "top quack quack" dǐng guā guā 顶 呱 呱 is supplied. Similarly, màn (màn) chī 慢（慢）吃 is a practically inevitable term once our textbook characters have managed their introductions and are seated for the important business of sharing a meal. A glance over the page for the previous entry will, however, bring students to the related yet lexically neglected màn qí màn qí 慢 骑 慢 骑 to tell a friend who's leaving on bicycle to ride carefully. Occasions for saying goodbye in this way would be common on any university campus, but in over a decade of teaching Chinese to American undergraduates, I've not noticed the expression in a dialogue.

I first met Jerome P. Keuper in 1994, when I was directing the Asian Studies Program at the University of Florida. It surprised me that a professor of nuclear physics, and the founder of the Florida Institute of Technology, was aware of the teaching materials being used in Chinese language programs throughout the United States. As Keuper described his research to produce an up-to-date handbook of Chinese idioms, I realized that the project grew from a lifelong engage-ment with the language and people, one that has inter-sected periodically with the reponsibilities of a full career. The finished work, completed mainly during the past five years, draws from materials published around the world about Chinese idioms and the spoken language. Browsing through *Chinese 1000* has refreshed

my memory of expressions I'd forgotten, and introduced me to a great many I'd not known. Of course, I
would expect it to boost the proficiency of my students.
For the newcomers most of all, I hope that the pleasure
of learning idioms will inspire them to make a lasting
commitment to the language.

Chén Měi Lì   Cynthia L. Chennault
陈　美　丽   Associate Professor,
                     Chinese Language and
                         Literature
                     University of Florida,
                     Gainesville, Florida, U.S.A.

Introduction .....

It may seem strange that a dictionary of colloquial and idiomatic
expressions in Mandarin Chinese should be compiled by an
American physicist. Especially so since that physicist has never had
an opportunity to live in a foreign country or take a course in the
Chinese language.

Of course I wish that I had had those opportunities. But perhaps all
was not lost in the sense that the years that I have devoted to
teaching myself the Chinese language, I have learned the hard way
where the "bones are buried". I have become a believer in the old
saying " you can't know a language if you don't know its idioms".
Chinese 1000 is designed to help you with those idioms I had to
struggle with, and at the same time help you enrich your own
fluency with the language.

All of us have our own reasons for embarking on the arduous
journey to learn Chinese. My fascination with the Chinese people
and their language had its origin in WW II. I had been sent to China
as an Intelligence Officer with the O.S.S. on a very small ship. En
route, time seemed to crawl. When we were almost within sight of
Calcutta, the crew mutinied. The mutiny was put down but we were
forced to go all the way back to Australia and leave the ship. By the
time I finally arrived at my destination I had had time to memorize a
complete box of 1000 Chinese character flash cards that I had
brought with me. And so began my lifelong romance with the
Chinese language.

This dictionary lists 1000 idiomatic and colloquial expressions in
Mandarin Chinese (called "guo yu" in Taiwan and "putonghua" in
mainland China.) Each expression entry is numbered and arranged
alphabetically using the Roman Pinyin system. Each expression is
also given in simplified Chinese characters followed by a translation
of the literal meaning. The figurative meaning in English is given
last, often in idiomatic English.

I based my selection of entries on many years of intensive home
study of Mandarin Chinese and six visits to the Republic of China

and the Peoples Republic of China. Most of the entries were selected from a review of the 69 books listed in the bibliography. (See Appendix A.) Many were suggested by Chinese friends and university students. Criteria for selection were (a) important, (b) interesting, (c) humorous, and (d) popular in the opinion of the Author and many reviewers.

Appendix B is a cross-indexing (English to Chinese). This index provides a complete listing of English code words and entry numbers for corresponding Chinese expressions in the dictionary. Each entry for a Chinese expression in the dictionary is numbered and listed alphabetically according to its pinyin syllables.

It should be fun and instructive for the student to memorize any number of these expressions to amaze, amuse, and impress one's Chinese friends and classmates.

An idiom has been described by one linguist (Xue Zhi Zhang 1988) as follows:

> A little spark of life and energy in our speech ...
> Diction deprived of idioms ... soon becomes tasteless, dull, and insipid.

Most good Chinese-to-English dictionaries abound with what might be called two word idioms but are in reality compound words. The population of this group is beyond the scope of this book but I have elected to include some of them for various reasons. Also I have tried to avoid including four word idioms that are readily available in the literature (see Bibliography).

Linguists generally distinguish between idioms and proverbs. The *Concise Oxford Dictionary of Proverbs* (Simpson 1982) defines a proverb as a " traditional saying which offers advice or presents a moral in a short or pithy manner". I have elected not to include proverbs, sayings, or axioms in this dictionary although some may have crept in for one reason or another.

Several comments are in order here regarding certain conventions about details of the entries in *Chinese 1000,* as follows:

1. Romanization. This is a system for representing the sounds of the Chinese characters using the Roman alphabet. Several older Romanizations, or transliterations, are known as Wade-Giles and Yale. However, *Chinese 1000* uses a system known as "pinyin" which translates as "spell sound".

In 1959 the Peoples Republic of China (P.R.C.) adopted pinyin as the official system. All school children in the P.R.C. are introduced to pinyin to teach correct pronunciation of the Chinese characters. The western press uses pinyin almost universally for proper Chinese names and places. The Republic of China (R.O.C.) has never officially adopted pinyin and continues to use the older systems. This dictionary uses the pinyin system.

2. Placing of tone marks (- ˊ ˇ ˋ). The reader will note that the tone mark is always placed over the vowel in the pinyin syllable. When there are two consecutive vowels it is placed over the first unless it is an "i" or a "u" in which case it is placed over the second vowel. A syllable without a tone mark carries a neutral tone.

3. Tone changes. In spoken Chinese, the tone of a syllable may change depending on the position of the syllable in a distinct sentence part. For example:

yī (one) in isolation has the first tone, but when it precedes a syllable with a fourth tone it becomes yí in the second tone. When yī precedes a first, second, or third tone it changes to yì in the fourth tone.

bù (not) is usually pronounced in the fourth tone. However, when it is followed by another syllable also in the fourth tone, it is changed to bú in the second tone.

It is important that the reader recognize these changes since they *are* followed in this dictionary.

Another important tone change, especially in speaking, but one which is *not* followed in this dictionary to avoid confusion is:

> If a third tone (ˇ) is followed by another third tone, the first one changes to a second tone. If there are three consecutive syllables in the third tone, the middle one changes to the second tone.

4. The suffix "er". In the Beijing area it is common practice to add "er" to many pinyin words. This is sometimes called the Beijing "r". When this is used as a suffix the spelling of the pinyin word may change but the meaning of the word does not change. The Beijing "r" suffix is *not* used in *Chinese 1000*.

This should not be confused with the use of this suffix in certain pinyin words where it does change the meaning. An example is zhè meaning "this". When "r" is added to make zhèr it means "here". The Chinese character for this suffix must be added accordingly.

5. Alphabetical Ordering of the Entries. The romanization of the entries gives the *pinyin* for each character as a distinct syllable. While the occurrence of compound terms within the expressions is not reflected by this system, students will more readily perceive the sounds of individual characters than would be the case in a string of unseparated transliterations. Also the entries follow a strictly alphabetical order, disregarding tone. For example:

bǎi bān huā yàng, which begins with a third tone, comes before bái dào (rén), which begins with a second tone.

Learners of Chinese may be unsure which tone they heard at the start of an expression. Also, because of tonal change under certain conditions as sketched above, a strictly alphabetical order has the advantage of consistency.

6. Entry Numbers and English Code Word Index. To ease usage by English speakers each expression entry is numbered. The user can select an English code word from the index in Appendix B and find corresponding entry numbers. By searching for entry numbers in the dictionary the user finds the simplified Chinese expression desired. This English code word index system is considered a valuable feature of *Chinese 1000*.

7. Simplified Chinese Characters. In an effort to increase the literacy of the population, the new Communist party in China in 1949 set about to simplify many of the Chinese characters. So far, about 2000 characters have been simplified in the P.R.C. However the simplified characters have never been officially adopted in the R.O.C. and Hong Kong.

It is common practice in the United States to use the traditional characters in teaching beginning Chinese and to bring in the simplified characters later in the first year. The rationale here is that it is much easier to go from the traditional to the simplified than *vice-versa*. This will then give the student exposure to both systems. *Chinese 1000*, intended as a second book or reference, uses the simplified characters throughout.

The 21st Century, soon upon us, has been called the "Pacific Century" because of the rapidly growing economic importance of China and the other Pacific Rim countries. Interest in the study of Chinese as a foreign language is expected to grow accordingly. It is my sincere hope that this modest dictionary of idiomatic and collo-quial expressions will, in some way, contribute to that growing interest. At the same time, I hope that it will add "a little spark of life" as you learn to speak the great language of the "Middle Kingdom."

Jié Ruì Gǔ Bó   Jerome P. Keuper, Ph.D.
杰 睿 古 柏   Melbourne Beach, Florida,
                                               U.S.A.

Dictionary .....

Idiomatic and Colloquial Expressions

Simplified Chinese Characters

Mandarin Chinese/English

A

1. ài chī bù chī
   爱 吃 不 吃
   (like eat, not eat)
   eat it or not as you please; I don't give a damn if you eat or
   not.

2. ài chū fēng tóu
   爱 出 风 头
   (love out wind head)
   to be a "show off"; like to show off

3. ài shàng
   爱 上
   (love above)
   to fall in love with

4. ài zuò shén me zuò shén me
   爱 做 什 么 做 什 么
   (like do whatever, do whatever)
   to do what one pleases; to suit oneself

B

5. **bǎ fàn wǎn gěi zá le**
    把 饭 碗 给 砸 了
    (to have rice bowl smashed)
    to have lost one's job

6. **bā jiǔ bù lí shí**
    八 九 不 离 十
    (eight nine not far ten)
    pretty close; about right

7. **bā miàn líng lóng**
    八 面 玲 珑
    (8 side exquisite)
    manage to please everyone; a popular guy; all things to all
        men

8. **bá miáo zhù zhǎng**
    拔 苗 助 长
    (help sprouts grow by pulling up on them)
    to have the wrong idea; to ruin something with excessive
        enthusiasm or impatience

9. **bǎi bān huā yàng**
    百 般 花 样
    (hundred sort flower kind)
    to pull all kinds of tricks

10. **bái dào (rén)**
    白 道 (人)
    (white road person)
    an honest law abiding person; a good guy; a "white hat"

11.   **bái fèi jīng shén**
白 费 精 神
(white waste strength)
all of one's effort went for naught; to plow sand

12.   **bái fèi kǒu shé**
白 费 口 舌
(white waste mouth tongue)
waste one's breath

13.   **bǎi huò gōng sī**
百 货 公 司
(one hundred merchandise company)
department store

14.   **bài jiā zi**
败 家 子
(fail house son)
to be a spend thrift of a family or group

15.   **bǎi kàn bú yàn**
百 看 不 厌
(one hundred look not dislike)
never tire of seeing (something)

16.   **bǎi kǒu mò biàn**
百 口 莫 辩
(hundred mouths unable argue)
protests of innocence in vain

17.   **bái miàn shū shēng**
白 面 书 生
(white face scholar)
egg head; nerd; scholar; sometimes inexperienced in life

18.   **bái pǎo yí tàng**
白 跑 一 趟
(white run one)
to make a fruitless trip

3

19. **bǎi sī bù jiě**
百 思 不 解
(hundred think not solve)
cannot figure out even after great thought

20. **bǎi tīng bú yàn**
百 听 不 厌
(hundred listen not dislike)
never tire of hearing something

21. **bái shǒu qǐ jiā**
白 手 起 家
(white hand raise house)
once poor, now rich; rags to riches; to start with nothing

22. **bái tóu dào lǎo**
白 头 到 老
(white hair arrive old)
to live together; married for an entire lifetime; a congratulatory wedding message

23. **bái (wàn) wú yì shī**
百 （万） 无 一 失
(100 (10,000) no one mistake)
nothing can possibly go wrong; no risk at all; 100% sure; in the bag

24. **bái xīn kǔ**
白 辛 苦
(white hard work)
to waste one's efforts

25. **bái yǎn kàn rén**
白 眼 看 人
(white eye look person)
to look down upon; despise; to turn up one's nose on someone

4

26. **bǎi zhàn bǎi shèng**
百 战 百 胜
(hundred battles hundred wins)
to always win

27. **bàn fēng bù diān**
半 疯 不 颠
(half crazy not crazy)
only appears crazy

28. **bàn gōng bàn dú**
半 工 半 读
(half work half study)
work part-time, go to school part-time; full-time student
        working part-time

29. **bàn jīn bā liǎng**
半 斤 八 两
(half catty eight ounce)
all the same; six of one, half dozen of another

30. **bàn lù chū jiā**
半 路 出 家
(half way go out house)
change profession; switch to a job for which one was not
        trained; become a monk or nun late in life

31. **bān nòng shì fēi**
搬 弄 是 非
(move do true false)
to gossip; make mischief

32. **bǎn qǐ miàn kǒng**
板 起 面 孔
(board get up face)
to stiffen; to keep a straight face; to become serious; to
        begin to be angry

5

33. **bàn shǒu xù**
     办 手 续
     (doing process)
     to go through formalities

34. **bàn tiān**
     半 天
     (half day)
     long time

35. **bàn tú ér fèi**
     半 途 而 废
     (half way then abandon)
     to give up; not finish something

36. **bàn sǐ bù huó**
     半 死 不 活
     (half dead not alive)
     neither dead nor alive; exhausted

37. **bāng dào máng**
     帮 倒 忙
     (help upset)
     to be more of a hinderance than a help

38. **bǎng shàng wú míng**
     榜 上 无 名
     (no name on the placard)
     fail an examination or competition

39. **bāng yí gè máng**
     帮 一 个 忙
     (help one help)
     to help one time; to do someone a favor

40. **bāo dǎ tīng**
     包 打 听
     (undertake inquiry)
     to be a "busy body"; a curious and inquisitive soul; to stick
     one's nose into other people's business

6

41. **bāo guǎn**
包 管
(keep manage)
safekeeping; I can assure you!

42. **bāo luó wàn xiàng**
包 罗 万 象
(contains twelve 10,000 images)
all embracing

43. **báo mǔ**
保 母
(swaddling cloth mother)
baby sitter; servant; housekeeper; guard

44. **bào qiàn**
报 歉
(hug sorry)
to be sorry; to regret

45. **bǎo quán miàn zi**
保 全 面 子
(keep whole face)
not lose face

46. **bào xǐ bu bào yōu**
报 喜 不 报 忧
(report happy not sad)
to "white wash" an investigation

47. **bào yuàn**
抱 怨
(embrace grudge)
to complain; grumble

48. **bǎo zhòng**
保 重
(insure heavy)
look after yourself; take care

7

49. **bèi dào ér chí**
背 道 而 驰
(back road then run)
to be out of line; run counter to

50. **Bèi duō fēn**
背 多 分   [This is a homophone of 贝 多 分]
(Beethoven)   [Common Chinese translation of his name.]
to memorize and get many points in school

51. **bēi hēi guō**
背 黑 锅
(carry on shoulder black pot)
to be made a scapegoat

52. **bèn dàn**
笨 蛋
(dumb egg)
stupid fellow

53. **bèn shǒu bèn jiǎo**
笨 手 笨 脚
(dumb hand dumb feet)
"all thumbs"; clumsy feet and hands

54. **bèn tóu bèn nǎo**
笨 头 笨 脑
(dumb head dumb brain)
to be stupid; slow witted

55. **bǐ bi jiē shì**
比 比 皆 是
(seen everywhere)
very abundant

56. **bǐ cǐ bǐ cǐ**
彼 此 彼 此
(in the same situation)
to be in the same boat; to be no better off than

57. bǐ fāng shuō
     比 方 说
     (compare square say)
     for example

58. biàn běn jiā lì
     变 本 加 厉
     (change original add strength or severity)
     to change to something greater than the original; to go
          further in a negative way

59. biàn bié shí fēi
     辩 别 是 非
     (know correct incorrect)
     tell right from wrong; truth from falsehood

60. biǎo lǐ rú yī
     表 里 如 一
     (outside inside as one)
     think and act in the same way

61. biāo xīn lì yì
     标 新 立 异
     (display new make different)
     to create something different and unusual

62. bié chū xīn cái
     别 出 心 裁
     (distinct produced heart tailored)
     to show originality

63. bié jù qíng qù
     别 具 情 趣
     (distinct possess charm)
     have a distinctive flavor or charm

64. bié kè qì
     别 客 气
     (don't be so polite)
     you are welcome; don't mention it; make youself at home

9

65. **bié nào**
别 闹
(don't be noisy)
be quiet; behave yourself; don't make trouble

66. **bié sòng**
别 送
(don't send)
you need not accompany me any farther (as a guest would
    say to a host upon leaving)

67. **bié shù yí zhì**
别 树 一 帜
(distinct set up a flag)
act independently; get out of a rut; set up one's own school

68. **bié wú cháng wù**
别 无 长 物
(don't nothing long things)
to have only the bare necessities

69. **bié yǒu yòng xīn**
别 有 用 心
(other possess motive)
to have ulterior motives

70. **bú ài shì**
不 碍 事
(not bother affair)
that's all right!

71. **bú bì jiè yì**
不 必 介 意
(don't care)
never mind

72. **bù chǐ**
不 齿
(not teeth)
despise; hold in contempt

10

73. **bù chī bái bù chī**
不 吃 白 不 吃
(not eat white no eat)
help yourself, it's already paid for

74. **bù chǐ xià wèn**
不 耻 下 问
(not shameful low ask)
to not feel ashamed to ask and learn from a subordinate or
    someone considered less knowledgeable

75. **bù cí láo kǔ**
不 辞 劳 苦
(not avoid hard work)
to take great pains; to spare no pain

76. **bù chū suǒ liào**
不 出 所 料
(not outside expect)
as expected

77. **bú cuò**
不 错
(not wrong)
not bad; that's right

78. **bú dà yě bù xiǎo**
不 大 也 不 小
(not big yet not small)
just right size

79. **bú dàn (rú cǐ) ... ér qiě**
不 但 （如 此）而 且
(not only (this)...but also...)
not only...but...

80. **bú dàng yì huí shì**
不 当 一 回 事
(not think one matter)
not regard as a matter of importance

11

81. **bù dǎ zì zhāo**
不 打 自 招
(not hit self tell)
confess without being pressed

82. **bú dào Huāng He xīn bù sǐ**
不 到 黄 河 心 不 死
(not reach Yellow River heart not death)
not stop until one reaches one's goal; refuses to give up
until all hopes are gone

83. **bù dé bù**
不 得 不
(no, but no no)
cannot but...; to have no choice; to have to

84. **bù dé liǎo**
不 得 了
(no grasp)
good heavens; how awful

85. **bù dé rén xīn**
不 得 人 心
(not gaining people's heart)
not enjoy popular support; be unpopular

86. **bù dēng dà yǎ zhī táng**
不 登 大 雅 之 堂
(not reaching elegant hall)
not appeal to refined taste

87. **bú èr jià**
不 二 价
(no second price)
fixed price

88. **bù fáng**
不 妨
(not interfere with)
might as well

12

89. bù fēn qīng hóng zào bái
不 分 青 红 皂 白
(not distinguish green red black white)
indiscriminately

90. bù gǎn dāng
不 敢 当
(not dare take)
to not deserve something; ie: flattery etc.

91. bù guǎn sān qī èr shí yī
不 管 三 七 二 十 一
(no matter 3 x 7 equals 21)
going to do it no matter what!

92. bù guán zěn me yàng
不 管 怎 么 样
(no matter what)
no matter what, in any case

93. bú guò rú cǐ
不 过 如 此
(not pass such)
just so so, mediocre

94. bù hǎo chī
不 好 吃
(not good eat)
taste awful (opinion)

95. bù hǎo yì si
不 好 意 思
(not good meaning)
to be embarrassed

96. bù huāng bù máng
不 慌 不 忙
(not agitated not busy)
calmly

13

97. **bú huì kè qi**
不 会 客 气
(will not be polite)
formal-response by a guest to a host who says "bie ke qi"

98. **bù jiǎ sī suǒ**
不 假 思 索
(not rely on thinking)
without hesitation or thinking

99. **bú jiàn bú sàn**
不 见 不 散
(not see not go)
don't leave until we meet; until we are all there

100. **bú jiàn de**
不 见 得
(not see)
not necessarily so

101. **bú jiàn tiān rì**
不 见 天 日
(not see sky day)
in seclusion; in misery; have a miserable life

102. **bù kě kāi jiāo**
不 可 开 交
(not able free intanglement or involvement)
can not free oneself from something undesirable; can not
get out of something

103. **bú (yào) kè qi**
不（要）客 气
(don't be so polite)
don't be so formal; don't "stand on ceremony," you're
welcome

104. **bù kě sī yì**
不 可 思 议
(not able think idea)
inconceivable; incredible

105. **bù láo ér huò**
不 劳 而 获
(not work still gain)
to get something for doing no work; something for nothing

106. **bù míng yì wén**
不 名 一 文
(not possess one cent)
penniless; without one cent to one's name, broke

107. **bù sān bú sì**
不 三 不 四
(not three not four)
out of place; inappropriate

108. **bù shǎo**
不 少
(not few)
quite a few

109. **bú shì shí fēn hǎo**
不 是 十 分 好
(not 10 points good)
satisfactory; not perfect

110. **bú shù fú**
不 舒 服
(not comfortable)
to not feel well

111. **bú sòng le**
不 送 了
(not see off)
don't bother to see me further" (guest on leaving). "excuse
me for not seeing you further" (host)

112. **bú wài hū**
不 外 乎
(not outside)
no more than

113. **bù wén bú wèn**
不 闻 不 问
(not hear not ask)
to show no interest in (something)

114. **bú xiàng huà**
不 像 话
(does not resemble language)
to go too far; beyond the limit

115. **bú xiè**
不 谢
(no thanks)
not at all (response to "thank you"), you're welcome

116. **bú yào dān xīn**
不 要 担 心
(not want burden heart)
don't worry

117. **bú yào jǐn**
不 要 紧
(not want tight)
don't worry about it; it doesn't matter; unimportant

118. **bú yào liǎn**
不 要 脸
(not want face)
shameless

119. **bú yòng**
不 用
(not use)
no need; not necessary

120. **bú yòng xiè**
不 用 谢
(not use thanks)
don't mention it; you are welcome; not at all

121.　bú zǎo le
　　　不　早　了
　　　(not early)
　　　it is getting late

122.　bú zěn me yàng
　　　不　怎　么　样
　　　(not impressive)
　　　it doesn't amount to much; nothing special; not very good

123.　bú zhì yú
　　　不　至　于
　　　(not reach to)
　　　not as bad as..., not so bad that...

C

124. **cái mào shuāng quán**
才 貌 双 全
(talent face pair complete)
to be both talented and handsome (beautiful)

125. **cài niǎo**
菜 鸟
(vegetable bird)
beginner; "tender foot" (Taiwan)

126. **cǎn bù rén dǔ**
惨 不 忍 睹
(miserable not bear look)
can not bear to see

127. **cǎo bāo**
草 包
(grass bundle)
someone who has no ablility

128. **chà bù duō**
差 不 多
(lack not much)
about the same; almost

129. **chā duì**
插 队
(cut into a line)
to cut into a line of people; to send high-school grads
to the countryside during the Cultural Revolution

130. chāi tái
拆 台
(pull away supportive)
embarrass one or cause one to lose face in front of others;
      hinder someone's work

131. chàng fǎn diào
唱 反 调
(sing opposite note)
disagree

132. chéng fēng pò làng
乘 风 破 浪
(to ride wind and waves)
to have a smooth trip; to overcome obstacles

133. chéng jiàn
成 见
(set views)
prejudice

134. chéng qiān shàng wàn
成 千 上 万
(set thousand set ten thousand)
tens of thousands

135. chéng qīn
成 亲
(become relatives)
to get married

136. chéng qún jié duì
成 群 结 队
(together group together teams)
in groups; in crowds

137. chéng xīn
诚 心
(sincere heart)
sincerely

19

138. chī bái fàn
吃 白 饭
(eat white rice)
to be a "good for nothing"

139. chī bǎo le
吃 饱 了
(eat full)
I have eaten enough

140. chī bù kāi
吃 不 开
(eat not open)
to be unpopular

141. chī bú xià
吃 不 下
(eat no down)
to not be able to eat anymore

142. chī cù
吃 醋
(eat vinegar)
to be jealous

143. chī dà guō fàn
吃 大 锅 饭
(eat big pot rice)
no competition; everyone is treated the same regardless of
       merit and performance

144. chī dòu fu
吃 豆 腐
(eat bean curd)
to flirt (opposite sex)

145. chī fàn le méi yǒu?
吃 饭 了 没 有
(have you eaten?)
a casual greeting

146. **chī jīng**
吃 惊
(eat alarm)
to be shocked, amazed

147. **chī kǔ**
吃 苦
(eat bitterness)
bear hardship

148. **chī kǔ nài láo**
吃 苦 耐 劳
(eat bitterness bear hardship)
suffer bitterness and endure hardship

149. **chī kuī**
吃 亏
(eat loss)
to be on the losing end; to get the worst of it

150. **chī láo běn**
吃 老 本
(eat old savings)
to live off of one's earlier gains

151. **chī lì**
吃 力
(eat strength)
strenuous, difficult

152. **chī ruǎn bù chī yìng**
吃 软 不 吃 硬
(eat soft not eat hard)
bully the soft, not the strong; amenable to persuasion

153. **chī ruǎn fàn**
吃 软 饭
(to eat soft rice)
to live off one's wife or girlfriend

154. chī sì fāng
吃 四 方
(eat 4 directions)
to be an opportunist

155. chī xián fàn
吃 闲 饭
(eat idle food)
to be a "good for nothing"; a "sponger"; a "goof off"

156. chī xiāng
吃 香
(eat fragrant)
be popular

157. chī yā dàn
吃 鸭 蛋
(to eat a duck egg)
to be "shut out"; fail to win any points

158. chī yī kàn èr yàn guān sān
吃 一 看 二 眼 观 三
(eat one look two eye see three)
to be on one's guard

159. chì zhò fēng yún
叱 咤 风 云
(command wind and clouds)
to be powerful; have great influence

160. chōu chū shí jiān
抽 出 时 间
(take out time)
to manage to find time

161. chōu kòng
抽 空
(pull vacancy)
to manage to find time; make time

162. chòu měi
臭 美
(stinking beautiful)
A curse on somebody who boasts or brags

163. chū chāi
出 差
(go out errand)
to be out of town on business

164. chū chǒu
出 丑
(reveal news)
to make a fool of one's self

165. chū fēng tóu
出 风 头
(go out wind head)
to like to be in the lime light

166. chū jiā
出 家
(leave home)
to become a monk

167. chū mén
出 门
(to go out of the door)
to be out of town; go on a journey

168. chū rù píng ān
出 入 平 安
(out in safely)
may you be safe on all your trips (a traditional holiday
        greeting)

169. chū shì le
出 事 了
(out thing)
something went wrong

23

170. chuán jiào
   传 教
   (transfer teach)
   do missionary work; to read the riot act to someone; to
     scold; to "bawl out"

171. chuān xiǎo xié
   穿 小 鞋
   (to wear tight shoes)
   to mistreat someone; to "feel the pinch"

172. chuī niú (pí)
   吹 牛 （皮）
   (blow cow skin)
   to brag, boast

173. chuò chuo yǒu yú
   绰 绰 有 余
   (ample have spare)
   more than needed

174. dà biàn
大 便
(big convenience)
to defecate

175. dǎ biān gǔ
打 边 鼓
(beat side drum)
to beat the drums for someone; to assist in helping or
    encouraging someone

176. dǎ bù tōng
打 不 通
(strike not through)
cannot get through (telephone)

177. dǎ chà
打 岔
(strike digression)
to interrupt

178. dǎ diàn huà
打 电 话
(strike electric speach)
make a phone call

179. dà diǎn shēng
大 点 声
(big dot sound)
to speak a little louder

180. **dà fā léi tíng**
大 发 雷 霆
(big issue thunder)
to fly into a rage

181. **dà hào**
大 号
(big number)
to deficate (Taiwan)

182. **dǎ hū**
打 呼
(strike breath)
to snore

183. **dǎ jiāo dao**
打 交 道
(hit relationship)
to deal with something or somebody

184. **Dà Lù**
大 陆
(big land)
Mainland China

185. **dǎ mǎ hū yǎn**
打 马 虎 眼
(hit horse tiger eye)
to do something carelessly and poorly

186. **dà nán rén zhǔ yì**
大 男 人 主 义
(big man)
the idea that a husband should be in charge; macho

187. **dǎ pò shā guō wèn dào dǐ**
打 破 砂 锅 问 到 底
(beat break pot ask arrive bottom)
to get to the bottom of something; never give up

188. **dà shì qíng**
大 事 情
(big matter)
something serious

189. **dà shuǎ zuǐ pí zi**
大 耍 嘴 皮 子
(big play mouth skins)
to be glib; to be a big talker

190. **dǎ tīng**
打 听
(beat hear)
to ask about; inquire about

191. **dǎ xiǎo suàn pán**
打 小 算 盘
(use a small abacus)
to be petty and scheming

192. **dà yì**
大 义
(big meaning)
general idea, careless, negligent

193. **dà yuē**
大 约
(big about)
about, almost

194. **dà zhe dǎn**
大 着 胆
(big courage)
to pluck up one's courage

195. **dà zuǐ ba**
大 嘴 巴
(big mouth)
a gossip; one who tells on others and reveals secrets

196. **dài lù mào zi**
戴 绿 帽 子
(wear a green hat)
to have a wife who is unfaithful

197. **dài màn**
怠 慢
(humble & slow)
I have treated you poorly (said to a guest leaving a party);
   an expression of courtesy

198. **dāi ruò mù jī**
呆 若 木 鸡
(stay as if wood chicken)
temporarily stunned; dumbfounded as a wooden chicken

199. **dān dang bù qǐ**
担 当 不 起
(responsibility withstand not)
not able to assume responsibility

200. **dān qiāng pǐ mǎ**
单 枪 匹 马
(single spear one horse)
single handed

201. **dān xīn**
担 心
(burden heart)
to worry; to bear; "carry on one's shoulder"

202. **dǎn zhàn xīn jīng**
胆 颤 心 惊
(gall tremble heart tremble)
to be terror stricken

203. **dāng chū**
当 初
(at that time begining)
in the first place

204. **dàng méi nà huí shì**
当　没　那　回　事
(consider no that matter)
to pay no attention to something; pretend nothing
    happened

205. **dào dǐ zěn me yàng**
到　底　怎　么　样
(arrive bottom how is it?)
so what will it be?

206. **dǎo méi**
倒　霉
(fall down molding)
unlucky; unfortunate

207. **dào tóu**
到　头
(fall down head)
to lay down one's head to sleep

208. **dào zāi cōng**
倒　栽　葱
(plant onion upside down)
to fall head first

209. **dào zhì**
倒　置
(to set up reversed)
to put the cart before the horse

210. ••••• **de huà**
••••• 的　话
[no literal translation]
• • • • • , so to speak [for emphasis]

211. **dé le**
得　啦
[no literal translation]
that's enough; pack it in

212. **děng deng**
等 等
(wait wait)
"etc"; and so forth

213. **děng jí le**
等 急 了
(wait hurry)
concern caused by waiting a long time

214. **dēng tuǐ**
蹬 腿
(stretched legs)
dead; "kicked the bucket"

215. **dī sān xià sì**
低 三 下 四
(low three down four)
humble; low; servile

216. **diàn dēng pāo**
电 灯 泡
(electric light bulb)
a chaperone

217. **diān pèi líu lí**
颠 沛 流 离
(tremble, fall, move and separate)
homeless and miserable

218. **diǎn xīn**
点 心
(a dot on the heart)
a snack; a small portion of food

219. **diāo nàn**
刁 难
(cunning difficult)
to make thing difficult for someone

220. **dǐng guā guā**
顶 呱 呱
(top quack quack)
very very good

221. **dǐng hǎo**
顶 好
(on top good)
the best

222. **dìng jū xià lái**
定 居 下 来
(decide live down)
to settle down

223. **dòng huǒ**
动 火
(to start fire)
to be angry

224. **dōng nán xī běi**
东 南 西 北
(east, south, west, north)
in all directions

225. **dòng nǎo jīn**
动 脑 筋
(move brain muscle)
use one's head

226. **dòng nù**
动 怒
(move anger)
to lose one's temper

227. **dòng shen**
动 身
(move body)
to leave (on a journey)

228. **dòng shǒu**
动 手
(move hand)
to begin doing (something)

229. **dòng tǔ**
动 土
(move dirt)
to break ground (new building etc.)

230. **dǒu qǐ lái le**
抖 起 来 了
(shake rise come)
to become rich or powerful; to feel as though one were
    sitting on top of the world; complacent

231. **dù rì rú nián**
度 日 如 年
(pass day as if year)
to have a miserable life

232. **dú sǐ shū**
读 死 书
(read dead books)
to read without digesting material

233. **duàn duan xù xu**
断 断 续 续
(break break continue continue)
intermittently; off and on

234. **duàn dùn**
断 顿
(skip meal)
to go hungry (no money)

235. **duì bù qǐ**
对 不 起
(can not raise (my head) to face you)
I'm sorry; excuse me

236. **duì bú zhù**
      对 不 住
      (can not face you and stay in that position)
      excuse me; I am sorry

237. **duì niú tán qín**
      对 牛 弹 琴
      (play the lute to the cows)
      to talk to someone who hasn't the faintest idea of what
          you are talking about.

238. **duō shēng guì zi**
      多 生 贵 子
      (hope you will have many honorable sons)
      a traditional wedding greeting

ε

239. **èr bǎi wǔ**
二 百 五
(250)
someone stupid or silly; (more popular in north China:
see "shi san dian")

240. **ér qiě**
而 且
(and moreover...)
moreover; what's more; but also; futhermore

241. **èr sǐ le**
饿 死 了
(hungry die)
to be "starving"; dying of hunger.

242. **ěr tīng bā fāng**
耳 听 八 方
(ear hear 8 directions)
to keep listening carefully

243. fā zi
发 紫
(to emit purple glow)
to be extremely popular (see "hong de fa zi")

244. fàn bú shàng
犯 不 上
(commit not on top of)
not worth doing

245. fān tiān fù dì
翻 天 覆 地
(turn over sky, turn over earth)
result of natural tragedy such as an earthquake,
        hurricane etc; earth shaking; big change in life

246. fāng biàn
方 便
(square easy)
convenient

247. fàng jià
放 假
(release leave)
take a vacation; on holiday

248. fàng pào
放 炮
(light fire cracker)
to criticize or embarrass someone; light fire cracker

249. **fàng qì**
放 弃
(put down through)
give up

250. **fàng qīng sōng**
放 轻 怂
(put relax)
take it easy

251. **fàng xīn**
放 心
(liberate heart, put down heart)
to take it easy; relax

252. **fēi cǐ bù kě**
非 此 不 可
(only this no possibility)
to have no choice

253. **fēi cháng**
非 常
(not usual)
extremely

254. **fēi jī chǎng**
飞 机 场
(air port)
to be flat chested (woman); airport

255. **fēi lǘ fēi mǎ**
非 驴 非 马
(not donkey, not horse)
neither fish nor fowl

256. **fēi mèi yǎn**
飞 媚 眼
(fly flatter eye)
girl flirts with boy

257. fèi xīn sī
费 心 思
(spend heart thought)
go to a lot of trouble

258. fēn shǒu
分 手
(separate hand)
to say goodbye

259. fēng feng yǔ yu
风 风 雨 雨
(wind and rain)
go through many difficulties; gossip

260. fēng liáng huà
风 凉 话
(wind cool speech)
someone who is "all talk"; someone who talks
                    sarcastically and irresponsibly

261. fēng liú
风 流
(wind flow)
amorous

262. fēng shuǐ
风 水
(wind water)
pseudo scientific method of decision making based on
    harmony with nature; "geomancy"

263. fēng tǔ rén qíng
风 土 人 情
(wind ground man condition)
local conditions and customs

264. fū chàng fù suí
夫 唱 妇 随
(husband sings, wife follows)
to have a harmonious married life

G

265. gāi nǐ le
该 你 了
(should be yours)
it's your turn

266. gǎi rì jiàn
改 日 见
(change date see)
see you later

267. gāi sǐ
该 死
(deserving death)
damn it! drop dead!

268. gǎi tiān
改 天
(change day)
some other time

269. gǎi tiān jiàn
改 天 见
(change day see)
see you later

270. gài zhāng
盖 章
(cover stamp)
to stamp a document

271. **gān bēi**
乾　杯
(dry cup)
bottoms up (a drinking toast)

272. **gǎn shí jiān**
赶　时　间
(chase time)
to be in a hurry

273. **gàn má**
干　吗
(do what?)
what to do?; what for?; what the heck (are you doing?)

274. **gǎn yā zi shàng jià**
赶　鸭　子　上　架
(chase a duck onto a perch)
force someone to do something beyond one's ability

275. **gǎn zuò gǎn wéi**
敢　做　敢　为
(dare do, dare be)
afraid of nothing

276. **gāng gang hǎo**
刚　刚　好
(just just good)
just right

277. **gāo bí zi**
高　鼻　子
(tall nose)
referring to a Caucasian person as "tall nose" or
        "big nose"

278. **gào bié**
告　别
(tell leave)
to say good-bye

39

279. gāo (gao) xìng (xing)
高 （高） 兴 （兴）
(high spirits)
delighted; pleased

280. gè bēn dōng xī
各 分 东 西
(each separate south west)
each goes his own way

281. gè gěi gè de
各 给 各 的
(each give each)
"go dutch"; each pays his own way

282. gē mén er (gēmer)
哥 们 儿 （哥们儿）
(brothers)
buddies

283. gē qiǎn
搁 浅
(run around shallow)
reach a deadlock

284. gè wèi
各 位
(each person)
everyone

285. gè yǒu suǒ cháng
各 有 所 长
(each one has what good)
each one has its own strengths and good points

286. gè zhǒng gè yàng
各 种 各 样
(each various each differences)
all kinds of things

40

287. **gěi tā yán sè kàn kan**
给 他 颜 色 看 看
(give him colors look)
teach him a lesson

288. **gōng píng**
公 平
(public fair)
fair; impartial

289. **góng xǐ fā cái**
恭 喜 发 财
(congratulations and may you make a lot of money)
a Chinese New Year's greeting

290. **gòng xiǎng tián lún**
共 享 天 伦
(together share heaven human relations)
to share happiness (between members of a family)

291. **góng zuò kuáng**
工 作 狂
(work crazy)
to be a workaholic; to have a one track mind

292. **gǒu niáng yǎng de**
狗 娘 养 的
(born of a dog's mother)
son-of a-bitch

293. **gù bù de**
顾 不 得
(look after not)
not be able to do something about

294. **gǔ wǎng jīn lái**
古 往 今 来
(old go new come)
off with the old, on with the new; time marches on;
        always gu bu de

295. guā hú zi
刮 胡 子
(shave beard)
to scold; to "chew out" someone

296. guài bù de
怪 不 得
(strange not)
no wonder

297. guàn mǐ tāng
灌 迷 汤
(pour in rice soup)
to charm someone with flattery

298. guān xì
关 系
(depend on relationship)
one's "connections" in high places for success

299. guān xīn
关 心
(shut heart)
to pay attention to; to care; to be concerned about

300. guàng jiē
逛 街
(wander street)
to go window shopping; go shopping

301. guàng yí guàng
逛 一 逛
(walk one walk)
to go window shopping; walk around

302. gūi gēn dào dǐ
归 根 到 底
(return root reach bottom)
in the final analysis

303. **guǐ gui suì sui**
鬼 鬼 祟 祟
(ghost evil spirits)
sneaking around

304. **gǔn chū qù**
滚 出 去
(roll away)
beat it! scram! get lost! go away!

305. **gǔn dàn**
滚 蛋
(roll egg)
bug out! scram! go away!

306. **gǔn kāi**
滚 开
(roll open)
go away! beat it! get lost!

307. **guǒ bù qí rán**
果 不 其 然
(results not this right)
as one might expect; sure enough

308. **guò jiǎng**
过 奖
(over praise) [in response to praise]
to flatter someone; "You flatter me!"

309. **guò shì le**
过 世 了
(passed life)
to die

310. **guǒ rán**
果 然
(certainly is)
indeed, certainly

43

311. guò yì bú qù
      过 意 不 去
      (pass mind not go)
      to trouble someone; to "put someone out"; very sorry

312. guò yǐn
      过 瘾
      (pass addiction)
      to enjoy oneself to the fullest

313. **hái chà de yuǎn**
还 差 得 远
(still lack far)
to still have a long way to go; i.e., to learn something
(usually an expression of modesty)

314. **hái hǎo**
还 好
(still good)
still OK! (response to "ni hao")

315. **hái ké yǐ**
还 可 以
(still OK)
so so; regular (response to "ni hao ma")

316. **hái (shì) na yàng ma?**
还（是）那 样 吗
(still the same way?)
greeting to an old friend; "how goes it"?

317. **hài xǐ**
害 喜
(injure happy)
pregnant (morning sickness)

318. **hái yǒu**
还 有
(still have)
in addition; moreover, still, futhermore; by the way

319. **háng kōng mǔ jiàn**
航 空 母 舰
(aircraft carrier)
a fat person; "fatso"

320. **hǎo jí le**
好 极 了
(good highest)
extremely good; excellent

321. **hǎo jiā huo**
好 家 伙
(good utensil)
my goodness, goodness gracious, holy mackeral!

322. **hǎo jiǔ bú (or méi) jiàn**
好 久 不 (没) 见
(good long time not see)
"long time no see"; haven't seen you for a long time

323. **hǎo le! hǎo le!**
好 了 ! 好 了 !
(good! good!)
enough! enough! or, all right! all right!

324. **hǎo nán chī**
好 难 吃
(good difficult eat)
tastes really bad (opinion)

325. **hǎo shì hǎo**
好 是 好
(good is good)
it's all right; good though it may be

326. **hǎo xiàng**
好 像
(good look resembles)
it seems

327. hǎo zài
好 在
(good at)
fortunately

328. hē xī běi fēng
喝 西 北 风
(drink west north wind)
to have only the north west wind to drink or eat; very poor

329. hēi bái jiǎng
黑 白 讲
(black white speak)
to say anything whether it is true or not

330. hēi dào (rén)
黑 道（人）
(black road person)
to be a dishonest person; a crook; a bad guy; a "black hat"

331. hēi shè huì
黑 社 会
(black society)
illegal gangster; mafia

332. hēi xīn
黑 心
(black heart)
to be a mean person

333. hěn hóng
很 红
(to be very red)
said of famous actor, artist, etc.

334. hěn huī xīn
很 灰 心
(very grey heart)
said of one who is discouraged, defeated, depressed

335. **hóng de fā zǐ**
红　得　发　紫
(red turn purple)
to be an extremely popular artist, actor, etc.; a "super star"

336. **hòu huì yǒu qī**
後　会　有　期
(later meet have time)
(we will) meet again someday

337. **hòu lái**
後　来
(later come)
later; later on (events in the past)

338. **hòu lái ne**
後　来　呢
(later come what)
what then?

339. **hú lǐ hú tú**
糊　里　糊　涂
(messed up)
confused

340. **hú shuó bā dào**
胡　说　八　道
(confused talk eight speak)
to talk nonsense

341. **hǔ tóu shé wěi**
虎　头　蛇　尾
(tiger head snake tail)
to begin with vigor but fail to follow through

342. **huó dòng**
活　动
(live move)
activity

343. **huà hǔ lèi quǎn**
画 虎 类 犬
(paint tiger resemble dog)
to fail to achieve what one intended to do

344. **huā huā gōng zǐ**
花 花 公 子
(flower flower lord's son)
"playboy"; "wolf"

345. **huā jiē**
花 街
(flower street)
red light district; "cat house" district

346. **huā píng**
花 瓶
(flower vase)
someone admired for beauty alone; for display

347. **huā qián mǎi qì shòu**
花 钱 买 气 受
(spend money buy trouble)
spend money but buy only annoyance

348. **huá qiáo**
华 侨
(Chinese living in a foreign country)
Overseas Chinese

349. **huà shé tiān zú**
画 蛇 添 足
(draw snake add feet)
superfluous; to guild the lily

350. **huā tiān jiǔ dì**
花 天 酒 地
(flower sky liquor ground)
to indulge in worldly pleasures; wine, women and song

351. **huā yuān wang qián**
花 冤 枉 钱
(spend unjustly money)
spend much money but get very little to show for it

352. **huài dàn**
坏 蛋
(bad egg)
a foul fellow; a bad guy

353. **huān hū**
欢 呼
(happy shouting)
to cheer; hail; acclaim

354. **huàn jù huà shuō**
换 句 话 说
(change sentence speak)
in other words...; that is to say...

355. **huáng niú**
黄 牛
(yellow cow)
one who scalps tickets; one who breaks a promise

356. **huáng sè xiǎo shuō**
黄 色 小 说
(yellow novels)
pornographic books

357. **huáng zhǒng rén**
黄 种 人
(yellow variety people)
members of the "yellow race"

358. **huì huà**
会 话
(meet talk)
dialogue, conversation

359. huí lai le ma?
回 来 了 吗
(come back?)
a polite recognition that one has returned

360. huí tóu jiàn
回 头 见
(turn head see)
see you later

361. huó gāi
活 该
(live should)
it serves you right!

362. huó jiàn guǐ
活 见 鬼
(alive see ghost)
nonsense; damn it

363. huǒ shàng jiā yóu
火 上 加 油
(fire top add oil)
add fuel to the fire; to make an angry person even angrier

364. huǒ xìng zi
火 性 子
(fire personality)
hot tempered

365. huò zhě
或 者
(or is)
or; perhaps; it may be; probably so

366. jì bú zhù
记 不 住
(remember not live)
can't remember

367. jì chéng chē
计 程 车
(count distance car)
a taxi

368. jī dàn lǐ tiāo gú tóu
鸡 蛋 里 挑 骨 头
(to find bone in egg)
to make trouble; to find fault; being picky

369. jī fēi gǒu tiào
鸡 飞 狗 跳
(chicken fly dog jump)
everyone is nervous; on edge

370. jī hán jiāo pò
饥 寒 交 迫
(hungry cold join force)
suffer from hunger and cold; poverty stricken

371. jī máo suàn pí
鸡 毛 蒜 皮
(chicken feathers garlic skin)
trifles; bit and pieces; odds and ends

372. **jī pí gē da**
鸡 皮 疙 瘩
(chicken skin bumps)
goose bumps (caused by fear, cold, or too much flattering)

373. **jiā chǒu bù kě wài yáng**
家 丑 不 可 外 扬
(home dirt cannot speak out)
to wash ones' dirty linen at home; to keep one's family
        problems private

374. **jià lián wù měi**
价 廉 物 美
(price cheap goods beautiful)
fine goods at low prices

375. **jiǎ miàn jù**
假 面 具
(false mask)
to be "two faced"; to talk out of "both sides of the mouth";
        to pretend to be a nice person

376. **jiā rén**
家 人
(house persons)
members of the family

377. **jiǎ yáng guǐ zi**
假 洋 鬼 子
(imitation foreign devil)
a Chinese who dresses or behaves like a foreigner

378. **jiā yóu! jiā yóu!**
加 油 ! 加 油 !
(add oil)
Step on the gas!; to ask the driver to hurry; a yell to
        cheer on the home team at a sporting event

379. jiā yóu jiā cù
加 油 加 醋
(add oil add vinegar)
to exaggerate

380. jià zi dà
架 子 大
(big hanger)
"put on airs"; pretend to be better than everyone else

381. jiàn fēng zhuǎn duò
见 风 转 舵
(see wind turn rudder)
to be an opportunist

382. jiàn guǐ
见 鬼
(to see ghost)
nonsense

383. jiàn nèi
贱 内
(humble inside woman)
a way to refer to your own wife in old China

384. jiàn pián yi jiù qiǎng
见 便 宜 就 抢
(see cheap then grab)
to take advantage of every opportunity

385. jiàn qián yǎn kāi
见 钱 眼 开
(see money eye open)
to beam joyfully when money comes in view

386. jiàn tiān rì
见 天 日
(see sky and sun)
to be relieved of an injustice

387. jiǎn xiàn chéng
拣 现 成
(pick up now complete)
to get something unearned

388. jiàn yàng xué yàng
见 样 学 样
(see who imitates whom)
to be a "copy cat"

389. jiǎn zhe pián yi le
拣 着 便 宜 了
(get cheap)
to get an advantage from something; to get a bargain

390. jiàn Zhōu gōng
见 周 公
(see the Duke of Zhou) [Historical figure praised by Confucious]
to doze; fall asleep (in class etc.)

391. jiǎng jiě yuan
讲 解 员
(explain person)
guide

392. jiáo cái liǎng zhī chuán
脚 踩 两 只 船
(feet step two boat)
to straddle two boats; to have one foot in each camp

393. jiāo tóu jiē ěr
交 头 接 耳
(hand over; ear join)
speak in each other's ears; whisper to each other

394. jiǎ zhuāng
假 装
(false pretense)
to pretend

395. jiě bù liǎo kě
解 不 了 渴
(solve can not thirsty)
unable to quench one's thirst; unable to satisfy one

396. jiē duǎn
揭 短
(expose defect)
find fault with

397. jiē fēng
接 风
(meet wind)
to offer dinner to one who has arrived after trip

398. jiè guāng
借 光
(borrow light)
excuse me for walking in front of you; please let me thru

399. jiē guō
揭 锅
(uncover the pot)
to reveal, give away

400. jiè guò
借 过
(borrow pass)
excuse me for walking in front of you; please let me thru

401. jiě nāng xiāng zhù
解 囊 相 助
(untie purse both help)
to donate money

402. jiě shǒu
解 手
(relieve hand)
to go to the bathroom; to urinate

56

403. jiē shǒu
接 手
(accept hand)
substitute for someone

404. jīn kǒu yù yán
金 口 玉 言
(gold mouth jade language)
silver tongued orator; a promise never to be broken

405. jìn kuài
尽 快
(finish fast)
as soon as possible

406. jǐn zhāng
紧 张
(tight stretch)
stressful, tense

407. jìn zuì fāng xiū
尽 醉 方 休
(completed drunk then stop)
to drink one's fill

408. jiù nà me bàn
就 那 么 办
(then that way do)
then let's do it that way

409. jiù shì le
就 是 了
(this is)
it certainly is; indeed; it is no doubt; that's that! that's all!

410. jiù shì shuō
就 是 说
(just is say)
that is; it means

411. jiǔ yǎng
久 仰
(long time look up to)
so pleased to meet you finally - formal, somewhat outdated

412. jiù yào
就 要
(just want)
soon, about to

413. jiù zhè yàng
就 这 样
(then this kind)
that's all! that's it!

414. jú nèi rén
局 内 人
(office inside person)
insider, privileged to know the inside information

415. jǔ qí bú dìng
举 棋 不 定
(raise chessman not fixed)
undecided, shilly-shally

416. jué wú jǐn yǒu
绝 无 仅 有
(for sure only have)
the one and only one

开

417. kāi chéng xiāng jiàn
开 诚 相 见
(open honest both see)
to speak sincerely and frankly

418. kāi dāo
开 刀
(open knife)
operate on; perform surgery

419. kāi kōng tóu zhī piào
开 空 头 支 票
(write empty head check)
to write a bad check; empty promise

420. kāi mén jiàn shān
开 门 见 山
(open door see mountain)
to not beat around the bush; to say what we mean

421. kāi wán xiào
开 玩 笑
(open play smile)
to joke; to "kid"

422. kāi xīn
开 心
(open heart)
to be happy; to make fun of someone

423. **kǎi zi**
凯 子
(rich guy)
big spender (usually spent on women)

424. **kàn bìng**
看 病
(see sick)
to see a doctor

425. **kǎn dà shān**
砍 大 山
(cut the big mountain)
"shoot the breeze"; "shoot the bull"; idle talk

426. **kàn lái kàn qù**
看 来 看 去
(look come look go)
looked at from one angle and another; look all around

427. **kàn nǐ shuō de**
看 你 说 的
(look you speak)
Oh, come on! Come off it! (don't be so courteous)

428. **kàn yàng zi**
看 样 子
(see the way)
it seems

429. **kàn zhe bàn**
看 着 办
(look do)
do only that which is necessary; do as you see fit

430. **kàn zǒu yǎn (le)**
看 走 眼 （了）
(look go eye)
to mistake one thing for another

431. **kǎo lǜ kǎo lǜ**
考 虑 考 虑
(consider, think over)
a positive response to a request [little or no intent to comply]

432. **kě ài**
可 爱
(worthy love)
cute

433. **kě bú shì ma**
可 不 是 吗
(perhaps not is?)
isn't that the truth!

434. **kě kǒu**
可 口
(please mouth)
delicious, tasty; to one's liking

435. **kè qi**
客 气
(guest air)
polite, formal

436. **kè wén**
课 文
(lesson language)
text

437. **kě xiào sǐ le**
可 笑 死 了
(able laugh die)
to be extremely funny; to die laughing

438. **kěn dìng**
肯 定
(sure sure)
it is certain that; for sure

439. **kǒng pà**
恐 怕
(afraid, afraid)
afraid [in the sense of being concerned but not "frightened"]

440. **kōng qián jué hòu**
空 前 绝 后
(empty before, no more after)
never before and never will again

441. **kǒu tóu**
口 头
(mouth head)
oral; verbal

442. **kǒu tóu chán**
口 头 禅
(mouth head language)
pet phrase

443. **kóu yǔ huà**
口 语 化
(mouth language speaks)
colloquial

444. **kū bí zi**
哭 鼻 子
(cry nose)
to cry; weep

445. **kū zào**
枯 燥
(dried dry)
dull, boring

446. **kuài shuō a**
快 说 啊
(quick speak...)
to get ready to speak; out with it!

447. lā dǎo
拉 倒
(pull fall down)
forget about it!

448. lā jī shí wù
垃 圾 食 物
(garbage food)
junk food

449. lā yìng gōng
拉 硬 弓
(to pull a stiff bow)
to force someone to do something unwillingly

450. lái bù jí le
来 不 及 了
(come not arrive)
can't be ready on time; can't make it; not enough time!

451. lái jiè shào yí xià
来 介 绍 一 下
(come introduce one time)
introduce someone

452. lǎn chóng
懒 虫
(lazy worm)
one who is very lazy

453. **láng bèi bù kān**
狼 狈 不 堪
(wolf miserable)
to be "up a tree"; to be "between a rock and a hard place";
        in a difficult situation; in a tight corner

454. **láng bài wéi jiān**
狼 狈 为 奸
(wolf and another animal gang together to make trouble)
several persons create mischief together

455. **láng xīng gǒu fèi**
狼 心 狗 肺
(wolf heart dog lung)
extremely mean person

456. **lǎo bàn**
老 伴
(old partner)
my old husband; my old wife

457. **láo bǎn**
老 板
(old board)
the boss

458. **láo bǎi xìng**
老 百 姓
(old 100 last name)
common people [not government or army officials, etc.]

459. **lǎo chù nǔ**
老 处 女
(old virgin)
an "old maid"

460. **lǎo gōng**
老 公
(old man)
husband

64

461. **láo jià**
劳 驾
(labor arrive)
excuse me for troubling you; a polite way to ask for
        a favor or to disturb someone; much obliged

462. **lǎo pó**
老 婆
(old women)
a common term for one's wife

463. **lǎo niǎo**
老 鸟
(old bird)
an experienced person; an "old hand" (Taiwan)

464. **lǎo yàng zi**
老 样 子
(old kind)
same as ever [a response to an inquiry about one's health, etc.]

465. **lǎo yóu tiáo**
老 油 条
(old oil stick)
a "slick operator"; one who knows how to handle things
                            and does not work hard

466. **lèi sǐ le**
累 死 了
(tired die)
dead tired

467. **léi shēng dà, yú diǎn xiǎo**
雷 声 大, 雨 点 小
(thunder big, rain small)
one's bark is bigger that his bite

468. **lì hài**
厉 害
(severe harmful)
really awesome; tough; formidable; can handle everything

469. **lǐ lùn**
理 论
(reason discuss)
theory

470. **lián huán huà**
连 环 画
(connect round picture)
comic strips or small books with pictorials for children

471. **liǎn pí hòu**
脸 皮 厚
(face skin thick)
to be immodest; thick skinned; no shame.

472. **liáng bàn**
凉 拌
(cool mix up)
to abandon something since nothing can be done about it

473. **liǎo bù de!**
了 不 得 !
(not getting)
amazing; wonderful; marvelous; wow!; gosh!;

474. **liǎo bù qǐ**
了 不 起
(not raise up)
amazing; wonderful, very very good, great

475. **liǎo jiě**
了 解
(finish solve)
to know; to understand

476. **liáo shèng yú wú**
聊 胜 于 无
(slightly better than nothing)
at least better than nothing; "something is something"

477. líng jī yí dòng
      灵 机 一 动
      (suddenly one move)
      to have a sudden "brainstorm"; get a good idea

478. líng láng mǎn mù
      玲 琅 满 目
      (gem jade full eye)
      a feast for sore eyes; a lot of stuff

479. líng líng suì suì
      零 零 碎 碎
      (zero fragments)
      odds and ends

480. lín shí
      临 时
      (arrive time)
      on a moment's notice; temporary

481. lìng wài
      另 外
      (others outside)
      other; besides; apart from

482. liú bù
      留 步
      (stay step)
      don't bother to see me out or come any further

483. liú luò
      流 落
      (flow fall)
      to wander about destitute

484. liú shén
      留 神
      (stay alert)
      pay attention to; to be on the alert

485. **lóng fēi fèng wǔ**
龙 飞 凤 舞
(dragon flies, phoenix dances)
flamboyant; with a running style (not necessarily bad)

486. **lǚ tú yú kuài**
旅 途 愉 快
(trip happy)
have a pleasant journey

487. **luàn jiǎng**
乱 讲
(messy speak)
to say anything [regardless of the truth or whether it makes sense]

488. **luàn qī bā zāo**
乱 七 八 糟
(mess seven eight awful)
to be a mess; in confusion

489. **luò shuǐ**
落 水
(fall into water)
fall in with the wrong crowd

490. **luò shuǐ gǒu**
落 水 狗
(dog falls into water)
one who is defeated

491. **luò tāng jī**
落 汤 鸡
(fall soup chicken)
to be thoroughly soaked (wet)

492. **luò yì bù jué**
络 绎 不 绝
(continuous not break)
in an endless stream

m

493. má fan nǐ
麻 烦 你
(trouble you)
excuse me for troubling you; (but would you please
    do something for me?); may I ask for a favor?

494. mǎ mǎ hū hū
马 马 虎 虎
(horse horse tiger tiger)
just so so; not good not bad

495. mǎ shàng
马 上
(on horseback)
immediately; at once; right away

496. mǎi mài rén
买 卖 人
(buy sell person)
a business man

497. mài lì
卖 力
(sell strength)
to be hard working; make an extra effort

498. mài liǎn
卖 脸
(sell face)
sell looks not body

499. **mài mìng**
      卖 命
      (sell life)
      to "sweat blood", to "work one's tail off"

500. **mài nòng**
      卖 弄
      (sell do)
      to show off

501. **mài qiào**
      卖 俏
      (sell pretty)
      to flirt [girl]

502. **mài rén qíng**
      卖 人 情
      (sell people love)
      to sell fellowship; to do favors

503. **mài sǎ**
      卖 傻
      (sell stupid)
      to pretend not to understand

504. **mài xiào**
      卖 笑
      (sell smiles)
      to be a prostitute

505. **mài yì**
      卖 艺
      (sell art)
      to be an acrobat; artist, etc.

506. **mǎi zuì**
      买 醉
      (buy drink)
      go on a drinking spree

507. **mài zuǐ (pí)**
卖 嘴 （ 皮 ）
(sell mouth (skin))
to brag; to talk cleverly

508. **mán bú zaì hū**
漫 不 在 乎
(full not care)
to care very little

509. **mǎn chéng fēng yǔ**
满 城 风 雨
(full city wind rain)
the city is full of rumors

510. **màn laí**
慢 来
(slow come)
take it easy; relax

511. **màn (màn) chī**
慢 （ 慢 ）吃
(slow (slow) eat)
enjoy your meal; "Bon Appetit"

512. **màn (màn) zǒu**
慢 （ 慢 ）走
(slow (slow) go)
take it easy; take care [said at seeing a guest off]

513. **mǎn miàn chūn fēng**
满 面 春 风
(full face spring wind)
to radiate happiness

514. **màn paǒ**
慢 跑
(slow run)
to jog

515. màn qí màn qí
慢 骑 慢 骑
(ride slow)   [a parting remark to one leaving on a bicycle]
ride slowly and safely

516. màn tiān yào jià
漫 天 要 价
(completely want price)
to price something unreasonably high

517. mǎn zuǐ yīng wén
满 嘴 英 文
(full mouth English language)
to speak only English

518. máng rén qí xiā mǎ
盲 人 骑 瞎 马
(a blind man on a blind horse)
heading for a disaster; blind leading the blind

519. máng shén me
忙 什 么
(busy what)
what's the rush?; what's the hurry?; what are you doing?

520. méi ān hǎo xīn
没 安 好 心
(not place good heart)
to have evil intentions

521. méi cháng gùo kǔ tóu
没 尝 过 苦 头
(not tasted bitter head)
one who is stubborn and does things his own way;
     inexperienced

522. méi cuò
没 错
(not mistake)
you're right! so do it!

523. **méi fá zi**
      没 法 子
      (no way)
      it can't be helped; no remedy

524. **méi guān xī**
      没 关 系
      (no concern)
      don't mention it; never mind; it doesn't matter

525. **méi jiàn gùo miàn**
      没 见 过 面
      (have not see face)
      haven't met before

526. **méi mén**
      没 门
      (no door)
      no alternative; no choice

527. **méi mìng de**
      没 命 的
      (not life...)
      to go "all out" to do something, even risking one's life

528. **méi rén wèi**
      没 人 味
      (no person taste)
      to be a person no one can tolerate; to be one who has no
          conscience; heartless

529. **méi shén me (shì)**
      没 什 么 (事)
      (not something)
      never mind; don't mention it; it's nothing; it doesn't matter

530. **méi xiǎng dào**
      没 想 到
      (not think arrive)
      unexpectedly; to one's surprise

531. méi xīn gān
没 心 肝
(no heart liver)
having no conscience; heartless

532. méi xīn méi fèi
没 心 没 肺
(no heart no lung)
having no conscience; heartless

533. méi xīn yǎn
没 心 眼
(no heart eye)
straight forward; frank

534. méi yǐng de shì
没 影 的 事
(no shadow something)
empty talk; nonsense

535. méi yǒu bái chī bái hē de
没 有 白 吃 白 喝 的
(no white eat, no white drink)
no free lunch

536. méi wán méi liǎo
没 完 没 了
(not finished not finished)
long winded; big talker

537. méng gǔ dài fū
蒙 古 大 夫
(mongolian doctor)
"quack doctor"

538. mí shàng
迷 上
(mad up)
to be enthusiastic about; crazy about (something)

74

539.   miàn bù gǎi sè
面 不 改 色
(face not change color)
to remain composed

540.   miàn zi guà bú zhù
面 子 挂 不 住
(face hang not stay)
to embarass someone; to cause someone to lose face

541.   miáo xiě
描 写
(draw write)
to describe; sketch

542.   mín zhǔ
民 主
(people chief)
democracy

543.   míng bai
明 白
(clear white)
understand; clear

544.   míng shèng gǔ jī
名 胜 古 迹
(famous scenic ancient spot)
scenic spots and historical sites

545.   míng xiǎn
明 显
(bright manifest)
clear; obvious

546.   mō bù zháo tóu nǎo
摸 不 着 头 脑
(touch not head)
to be perplexed; at a loss

547. **mǒ hēi**
抹 黑
(apply black)
to blacken one's name

548. **mó jiān jiē zhǒng**
摩 肩 接 踵
(touch shoulder touch heels)
rub shoulders with people in a stream of people; jostle
each other in a crowd of people

549. **mò míng qí miào**
莫 名 其 妙
(no naming its strangeness)
not able to make heads or tails of something; "stumped"

550. **mù dèng kǒu dāi**
目 瞪 口 呆
(eye stare mouth stupid)
stupified; stunned

551. **mù tóu rén sì de**
木 头 人 似 的
(wood head person look like)
person with expressionless face; "poker face"

552. **mǔ yè chā**
母 夜 叉
(female night cross)
a very mean person (female); a bitch

N

553. ná de qǐ fàng de xià
拿 得 起 放 得 下
(take up put down)
to be able to cope with any situation

554. nǎ de huà
哪 的 话
(where is the talk?)
come on! who says so! not at all! [response to a
    compliment]

555. nà duǒ hǎo
那 多 好
(that much good)
that's great! how nice!

556. nǎ lǐ, nǎ lǐ
那 里, 那 里
(where where)
polite way to respond to a compliment

557. ná shǒu (hǎo xì)
拿 手 (好 戏)
(take hand good show)
to be good at

558. nà (kě) tài hǎo le
那 (可) 太 好 了
(that (certainly is) too good)
that's great! fine! OK!

559. **nán chī**
难 吃
(difficult tasting)
tastes bad [opinion]

560. **nán chī sǐ le**
难 吃 死 了
(hard eat die)
food is awful

561. **nán dào**
难 道
(hard to say)
do you mean to say that? it really has to be?

562. **nán kàn**
难 看
(difficult to look at)
ugly

563. **nán tián běi xián**
南 甜 北 咸
(South sweet, North salty)
people in southern China like sweet food, in northern
        China they like salty food; people differ in their
                                                tastes

564. **nán tīng**
难 听
(difficult to listen to)
sounds terrible

565. **nào téng**
闹 腾
(noise up)
noisy beehive of activity

566. **nào (le) xiào huà**
闹 （ 了 ） 笑 话
(made a joke)
make a dumb mistake and be embarassed

78

567. nào zhe wán
闹 着 玩
(made play)
to do something for fun; just kidding!

568. nèi bǐ shēng yì huáng le
那 笔 生 意 黄 了
(that pen business yellow)
the deal is off

569. nǐ duō dà le
你 多 大 了
(you how big?)
how old are you?

570. nǐ kàn zěn me yàng
你 看 怎 么 样
(you look what?)
what do you think?

571. nǐ shì nǎ ér (rén)?
你 是 哪 儿 （ 人 ）
(You are from where person?)
What country are you from? Where did you come from
     (area)?

572. nǐ tài hǎo le
你 太 好 了
(you too good)
you are very nice

573. nǐ tài kè qì le
你 太 客 气 了
(you too polite)
you are too kind, too polite

574. nǐ wèi
腻 味
(sick of taste)
to be "fed up"; disgusted

79

575. nǐ zěn me le
你 怎 么 了
(you what?)
what's wrong with you?

576. niàn bái zì
念 白 字
(read white character)
to read a character incorrectly

577. nián huá xū dù
年 华 虚 度
(years times blank spend)
to waste one's life

578. niàn jīng
念 经
(read classics)
to "harp" on something; to "nag"

579. nín nǎr wèi?
您 哪 位
(in what place are you)
telephone talk for "who are you"?

p

580. **pà lǎo pó**
怕 老 婆
(afraid of old woman)
to be afraid of one's wife [the "old lady"]

581. **pà qián pà hòu**
怕 前 怕 後
(to be afraid of front and back)
to be afraid of everything; to worry too much

582. **pāi mǎ pì**
拍 马 屁
(pat horse's rear end)
to flatter

583. **pàng dū dū de**
胖 嘟 嘟 的
(fat)
chubby; fat

584. **pǎo lái pǎo qù**
跑 来 跑 去
(run come run go)
to run around

585. **pǎo mǎ**
跑 马
(run horse)
to have a wet dream; to have a horse race

586. pào mǎ zi
泡 马 子
(soak horse)
to hang around with girls

587. pāo mèi yǎn
抛 媚 眼
(throw flatter eye)
girl flirts with boy

588. pèng bù qǐ
碰 不 起
(touch not)
to be touchy; thin skinned; super sensitive; not mess with

589. piàn kè jiù huí lái
片 刻 就 回 来
(quarter slice then return)
to be back in a moment; to be right back

590. piào liàng
漂 亮
(bleach bright)
attractive, beautiful [applies to things or women]

591. píng ān
平 安
(even peace)
peaceful; at peace

592. pò bù jí dài
迫 不 及 待
(urgent not at the moment wait)
too impatient to wait

593. pò fèi, pò fèi!
破 费, 破 费
(break fee)
said by a dinner guest at a restaurant or recipient of a gift:
    "you shouldn't have spent so much money!"

594.   pò guàn zǐ
破 罐 子
(broken jar)
unchaste woman; a physical wreck

595.   pò xié
破 鞋
(broken shoe)
loose woman; unchaste woman

596. qí hǔ nán xià
骑 虎 难 下
(ride tiger difficult to get off)
to have a tiger by the tail; to feel difficulty in an enterprise
      that one has undertaken

597. qǐ jū
起 居
(rise live)
get up and live one's normal lifestyle

598. qǐ mǎ
起 码
(start scale)
at least

599. qī shàng bā xià
七 上 八 下
(7 up 8 down)
an unsettled state of mind; agitated; perturbed

600. qí shí
其 实
(truth)
as a matter of fact; actually

601. qī shí èr háng
七 十 二 行
(72 rows)
all sorts of occupations; in every conceivable line of work

84

602. qí xiā mǎ
      骑 瞎 马
      (ride blind horse)
      to do something aimlessly

603. qiān chā wàn bié
      千 差 万 别
      (1,000 different 10,000 different)
      differ in many ways

604. qiān wàn
      千 万
      (1,000 - 10,000)
      by all means; to be sure to; surely

605. qiāo dìng le
      敲 定 了
      (strike fixed)
      it's a deal; it's settled then

606. qiāo zhú gàng
      敲 竹 杠
      (hit bamboo pole)
      to swindle someone

607. qiè fū zhī tòng
      切 肤 之 痛
      (close skin pain)
      heartfelt sorrow

608. qīn zì dòng shǒu
      亲 自 动 手
      (oneself move hand)
      to do something in person

609. qǐng kè
      请 客
      (invite guest)
      invite someone for a meal

610. qǐng nǐ zǒu lù
请 你 走 路
(please walk)
"Take a walk." "You're fired!"

611. qǐng wèn
请 问
(please ask)
excuse me (a polite way to propose a question)

612. qíng xíng zěn me yàng
情 形 怎 么 样
(situation what ?)
What's going on? How are things? What's up?

613. qǐng yuán liàng
请 原 谅
(please excuse)
please forgive me

614. qióng guāng dàn
穷 光 蛋
(poor smooth egg)
said of one who has no money

615. qióng shuō ge méi wán
穷 说 个 没 完
(continue talk not finish)
non stop talking

616. qiú jiào
求 教
(request teaching)
ask for advice

617. qiú nǐ jiàn shì
求 你 件 事
(beg you one thing)
Could you do me a favor?

618. qiú xié
球 鞋
(ball shoe)
sneakers

619. quán luàn le
全 乱 了
(complete mess)
to be in total confusion

620. quán xīn quán yì
全 心 全 意
(complete heart complete idea)
with great determination

R

621. ràng kāi
让 开
(let open)
get out of the way!

622. rào kǒu lìng
绕 口 令
(twist mouth order)
tongue twister

623. ráo mìng
饶 命
(pardon life)
don't kill me; don't hurt me

624. rào zuǐ
绕 嘴
(coil mouth)
difficult to say

625. rè mén
热 门
(hot door)
in great demand; popular

626. rè xiàn diàn huà
热 线 电 话
(hot line call)
a "hot line" telephone for getting through right away
without waiting - often used by heads of state.

627. rè xīn
热 心
(hot heart)
enthusiastic

628. rèn bù chū lái
认 不 出 来
(recognize not come out)
beyond recognition

629. rěn bú zhù
忍 不 住
(stand not live)
can not help doing something

630. rén miàn shòu xīn
人 面 兽 心
(man face animal heart)
a "wolf in sheeps clothing"

631. rén rén
人 人
(people people)
everyone

632. rén shān rén hǎi
人 山 人 海
(people mountain people ocean)
a sea of people; a crowd

633. rèn zì
认 字
(recognize word)
to know the Chinese characters; to be literate.

634. rú rì zhōng tiān
如 日 中 天
(as sun mid day)
to be like the sun at high noon; to ride on the crest of
success; to be very influential

635.　rú yuàn yǐ cháng
　　　如　愿　以　偿
　　　(as wish to reach)
　　　to succeed in getting what one wanted

636.　ruǎn gǔ tóu
　　　软　骨　头
　　　(soft bone)
　　　to be weak; cowardly

S

637. sān bā (xī xī)
三 八 (兮 兮)
(three eight)
to act crazy or silly (usually girl)

638. sàn bù
散 步
(break up step)
to take a walk or a stroll

639. sān tóu liù bì
三 头 六 臂
(three heads six arms)
superhuman

640. sān xīn èr yì
三 心 二 意
(three hearts two ideas)
indecisive; can't make up one's mind

641. sān yán liǎng yǔ
三 言 两 语
(three words, two remarks)
In a few words; in short

642. shà fèi kǔ xīn
煞 费 苦 心
(spend bitter heart)
painstakingly; laboriously; to "rack one's brains"

643. **shā jī jǐng hóu**
杀 鸡 儆 猴
(kill chicken frighten monkey)
to punish someone as a warning to others

644. **shǎ tóu shǎ nǎo**
傻 头 傻 脑
(stupid head stupid brain)
foolish looking; rattle brained

645. **shān qīng shuǐ xiù**
山 青 水 秀
(green hills and clear waters)
picturesque country scene

646. **shān qióng shuǐ jìn**
山 穷 水 尽
(mountains end water ends)
"at the end of one's rope"; to be at wit's end

647. **shān shuǐ huà**
山 水 画
(mountain water painting)
landscape painting

648. **shàng bān**
上 班
(up shift)
go on duty; work

649. **shāng fēng**
伤 风
(hurt wind)
catch cold

650. **shàng jiē**
上 街
(on the street)
go shopping

651. **shàng yī hào**
上 一 号
(go number one)
go to restroom to urinate

652. **shě bù dé**
舍 不 得
(part with not)
to hate to part with

653. **shēn bù yóu jǐ**
身 不 由 己
(body not follow self)
involuntarily; in spite of one's self

654. **shén me fēng bǎ nǐ chūi laí le?**
什 么 风 把 你 吹 来 了
(what wind blow you here?)
how come you are here? (half teasing half polite to a
                                                    friend)

655. **shén me shì**
什 么 事
(what thing?)
What's up? ; What's going on?

656. **shēng lóng huó hǔ**
生 龙 活 虎
(born dragon live tiger)
to be full of vigor and vitality; forceful

657. **shēng mǐ chéng shú fàn**
生 米 成 熟 饭
(the rice is already cooked)
what's done is done; no use crying over spilt milk; already
                                                            decided

658. **shēng qì**
生 气
(born angry)
to be angry; get mad

93

659. **shēng qì bó bó**
生 气 勃 勃
(born spirit active)
full of life; alive and kicking; dynamic and vigorous

660. **shì fēi tí**
是 非 题
(correct incorrect question)
a true or false question; (ie., on a test)

661. **shì jiè wén míng**
世 界 闻 名
(world hear name)
world famous

662. **shì lì yǎn**
势 利 眼
(power benefit eyes)
to do only that which is to one's advantage

663. **shí ná jiǔ wěn**
十 拿 九 稳
(ten take nine firm)
nine chances out of ten; 90% sure; in the bag

664. **shì nà yàng ma?!**
是 那 样 吗 ?!
(Yes that way?!)
is that so?!

665. **shì qióng guāng dàn**
是 穷 光 蛋
(poor nothing egg)
very poor

666. **shì qù**
识 趣
(know interesting)
to be tactful

667. shí quán shí měi
十 全 十 美
(ten complete ten beautiful)
to be perfect in everyway; leave nothing to be desired

668. shí sān diǎn
十 三 点
(13 points)   [see erbai wu]
to act crazy or silly (more popular in South China)

669. shì shí
事 实
(matter real)
fact

670. shí wàn huǒ jí
十 万 火 急
(ten ten thousand fire hurry)
extremely urgent

671. shī xìn
失 信
(lost honesty)
to break one's promise

672. shǐ xìng zi
使 性 子
(act temperament)
to lose one's temper

673. shì zhè yàng zi
是 这 样 子
(is this kind)
that's right!

674. shì zěn me huí shì ?
是 怎 么 回 事
(is what thing)
what happened?

675. shǐ zì
识 字
(know characters)
to be able to read Chinese; [see "ren zi"]

676. shī zǐ dà kāi kǒu
狮 子 大 开 口
(lion big open mouth)
ask too high a price

677. shí zì lù kǒu
十 字 路 口
(cross roads)
to hesitate; to be at the cross roads; the critical moment

678. shòu bù liǎo
受 不 了
(bear not)
unable to bear; can not endure; can't stand it!

679. shòu qì
受 气
(receive air)
suffer an injustice; take the blame

680. shǒu qiǎo
手 巧
(hand nimble)
skillful

681. shōu shí
收 拾
(collect, gather)
to pack up; get one's things ready; to put in order; to "get
    even" with someone; to "fix" someone

682. shǔ mǐ ér chuī
数 米 而 炊
(count rice cook)
to count rice grains before cooking; to be extremely poor

683. **shuǎ huā zhāo**
耍 花 招
(play flower tricks)
to play tricks

684. **shuǎ pín zuǐ**
耍 贫 嘴
(play poor mouth)
to talk nonsense; gabble; chatter; silly talk

685. **shuì guò tóu**
睡 过 头
(sleep over head)
to oversleep

686. **shuì lǎn jiào**
睡 懒 觉
(sleep lazy)
sleep in; get up late

687. **shuǐ tǔ bù fú**
水 土 不 服
(water soil not obey)
not accustomed to the climate of a new place; not
acclimated

688. **shuì yí jiào**
睡 一 觉
(sleep one sleep)
take a nap

689. **shùn biàn**
顺 便
(pass convenient)
in passing; when it's convenient; at the same time

690. **shùn lù**
顺 路
(pass road)
on the way; convenient; not out of the way

691. **shuō bú shàng lái**
      说 不 上 来
      (speak not up come)
      not able to say exactly

692. **shuō dōng dào xī**
      说 东 道 西
      (speak east speak west)
      to ramble in talking

693. **shuō hǎo de**
      说 好 的
      (to say OK)
      it is promised; it's a deal!

694. **shuō (qǐ) lái**
      说 (起) 来
      (talk come up...)
      in that case...

695. **shuō lái shuō qù**
      说 来 说 去
      (speak come speak go)
      to say something over and over again

696. **shuō mèng huà**
      说 梦 话
      (talk dream speach)
      to talk in one's sleep; to say something unrealistic

697. **shuō shì zhè me shuō**
      说 是 这 么 说
      (say is how come say)
      that's what people say; although people take it that way yet

698. **sì fēn wǔ liè**
      四 分 五 裂
      (four split five split)
      to be all split up

98

699. **sì miàn bā fāng**
四 面 八 方
(four sides eight directions)
on every side; all around

700. **sǐ qù huó lái**
死 去 活 来
(die go life come)
to be half dead

701. **sòng hóng bāo**
送 红 包
(give red envelope)
to bribe someone; to give a gift of money on Chinese New
Year's Day

702. **suàn le! suàn le!**
算 了！算 了！
(calculate)
Forget it! Never mind! It doesn't matter.

703. **suí biàn nǐ**
随 便 你
(follow convenience you)
as you wish; it's up to you; at your pleasure

704. **suí bō zhú liú**
随 波 逐 流
(follow wave follow flow)
drift with the tide; go with the crowd

705. **suí xīn suǒ yù**
随 心 所 欲
(follow heart as wish)
to have one's own way; do as one pleases

706. **suí yù ér ān**
随 遇 而 安
(follow meet the peace)
to feel at home anywhere; to be adaptable

99

7

707. tā hěn hóng
      他 很 红
      (to be very red)
      said of a famous actor, artist, etc.

708. tā hěn huī xīn
      他 很 灰 心
      (very gray heart)
      someone who is discouraged or defeated

709. tā hóng de fā zǐ
      他 红 得 发 紫
      (a person is so red he is beginning to look purple)
      to become a superstar (singer, actor, etc.)

710. tái bù qi tóu lái
      抬 不 起 头 来
      (raise up can not head come)
      to fail in something and not be able to face relatives and
          friends

711. tài hǎo le
      太 好 了
      (too good!)
      wonderful, that's great!

712. tài kè xì le
      太 客 气 了
      (too guest air)
      you are too polite

713. **tài kōng fēi xíng rén**
太 空 飞 行 人
(very empty fly go person)
astronaut

714. **tài má fán nǐ le**
太 麻 烦 你 了
(too much trouble you)
sorry to have troubled you so much

715. **tài yí hàn**
太 遗 憾
(too loss sorry)
too bad...what a pity

716. **tán hǔ sè biàn**
谈 虎 色 变
(talk tiger color change)
to turn pale at the mention of something terrible

717. **tán huà**
谈 话
(talk speech)
to chat; talk

718. **tǎo jià huán jià**
讨 价 还 价
(ask price change price)
to bargain over prices

719. **tián bù mǎn**
添 不 满
(fill not full)
can't fill up; never satisfied

720. **tiān liàng**
天 亮
(sky brightens)
day breaks

101

721. **tiān má fán**
添 麻 烦
(add trouble)
to trouble someone

722. **tiān na!**
天 哪！
(sky)
Good Lord! God! Gosh!

723. **tiān táng**
天 堂
(sky hall)
heaven

724. **tiān xiǎo dé**
天 晓 得
(heaven knows)
God knows! Who knows!

725. **tiāo dēng yè zhàn**
挑 灯 夜 战
(raise light night fight)
to burn the midnight oil

726. **tiáo pí**
调 皮
(mix skin)
to be naughty

727. **tiě fàn wǎn**
铁 饭 碗
(iron rice bowl)
one's steady job with government, party, army etc.

728. **tiě gōng jī**
铁 公 鸡
(iron male chicken)
miser; tight wad; stingy person

729. **tiě mǎ**
铁 马
(iron horse)
bicycle

730. **tǐng bàng**
挺 棒
(very excellent)
very good

731. **tīng shuō**
听 说
(hear say)
heard it said that; it is reported that

732. **tīng tiān yóu mìng**
听 天 由 命
(listen sky let life)
trust to luck; submit to the will of Heaven

733. **tíng tíng zǒu zǒu, zǒu zǒu tíng tíng**
停 停 走 走, 走 走 停 停
(stop go, go stop)
sometimes it works, sometimes it doesn't; to work
    intermittently (clock etc.)

734. **tóng chuāng**
同 窗
(share window)
classmates, school mates

735. **tòng kuài**
痛 快
(hurt fast)
straight forward; outspoken; to one's heart's content

736. **tōng xiāo dá dàn**
通 宵 达 旦
(throughout night reach dawn)
all night long

737. tōu jī mō gǒu
偷 鸡 摸 狗
(steal chicken touch dog)
to be a petty thief; dishonest

738. tōu kàn
偷 看
(steal look)
take a peek

739. tōu zuǐ
偷 嘴
(steal mouth)
to steal food, eat without permission

740. tǔ tóu tǔ nǎo
土 头 土 脑
(soil head soil brain)
a "country bumpkin"; a "hick"

W

741. **wài biǎo shàng**
外 表 上
(outside on)
on the surface; superficially

742. **wāi dǎ zhèng zháo**
歪 打 正 着
(crooked strike right place)
to score a lucky hit

743. **wài zǐ**
外 子
(outside person)
as a wife might refer to her husband

744. **wán dàn**
完 蛋
(finish egg)
Damn! We're finished!

745. **wán le**
完 了
(finish)
there is no hope

746. **wán nòng**
玩 弄
(play tease)
make fun of; play dirty tricks

747. wán wán le
玩 完 了
(play finish)
the game is over; time to quit

748. wàn yī
万 一
(ten thousand one)
in case

749. wáng bā dàn
王 八 蛋
(turtle egg)
S.O.B.

750. wàng chén mò jí
望 尘 莫 及
(see dust never reach)
to fall far behind

751. wàng chuān shuāng yǎn
望 穿 双 眼
(see through pair eyes)
anxious to see or have something

752. wàng dōng wàng xī
望 东 望 西
(look east look west)
look all around

753. wǎng lái
往 来
(go come)
to keep in touch with a friend

754. wàng méi zhǐ kě
望 梅 止 渴
(see plum stop thirst)
imagined satisfaction

755. **wàng yáng xīng tàn**
望 洋 兴 叹
(see ocean promote sigh)
to be frustrated in trying to do something difficult and sigh
in despair

756. **wéi de shì**
为 得 是
(for to be)
in order to; because; so as to

757. **wéi nǐ shì wèn**
唯 你 是 问
(only you is ask)
I hold only you responsible (for this)

758. **wēn bǎo**
温 饱
(warm full)
to have just enough to wear and eat; to be very poor

759. **wèn cháng wèn dǔan**
问 长 问 短
(ask long ask short)
to ask all kinds of questions; to show care

760. **wèn dǎo**
问 倒
(ask fall down)
to "stump"; "puzzle" (someone); beats me; I don't know

761. **wèn hǎo**
问 好
(ask good)
to give one's regards to; to say hello to

762. **wén máng**
文 盲
(word blind)
to be illiterate

763. **wěn zhā wěn dǎ**
稳 扎 稳 打
(steady secure steady hit)
to do things steadily and surely

764. **wǒ bú gàn le**
我 不 干 了
(I not do)
quit!

765. **wǒ fú nǐ le**
我 服 你 了
(I submit to you)
You convinced me

766. **wǒ lái**
我 来
(I come)
let me do it

767. **wǒ meí bǎ wò**
我 没 把 握
(not hold grasp)
I am not sure

768. **wǒ xià chē le**
我 下 车 了
(I down car)
I don't want to do this anymore; I quit!; I want to get down
    from a car

769. **wǒ zì jǐ lái**
我 自 己 来
(I myself come)
let me do it myself

770. **wǔ hú sì hǎi**
五 湖 四 海
(five lakes, four seas)
every corner

771.   **wǔ sì yùn dòng**
五 四 运 动
(5 - 4 movement)
The May Fourth Movement in China, 1919

772.   **wú suǒ wèi**
无 所 谓
(no what tell)
to make no difference; it doesn't matter; anything is fine; I
    do not care

773.   **wú yǐng wú zōng**
无 影 无 踪
(no shadow no trace)
without a shadow; without a trace; to disappear

774.   **wū zéi chē**
乌 贼 车
(squid car)
a car that spews out exhaust pollution resembling the
    action of a squid

x

775. xǐ bìng
喜 病
(happy sickness)
pregnant

776. xǐ chū wàng wài
喜 出 望 外
(happy out look outside)
unexpected happiness

777. xǐ dài gāo mào zǐ
喜 戴 高 帽 子
(like to wear tall hat)
to enjoy vain compliments

778. xí guàn yòng fǎ
习 惯 用 法
(customed method)
idiomatic

779. xī kè xī kè
稀 客 稀 客
(rare guest rare guest)
you seldom come

780. xǐ qì yáng yáng
喜 气 洋 洋
(happy air ocean ocean)
very happy

781. xí yǐ wéi cháng
习 以 为 常
(used to as always)
to be used to

782. xià bān
下 班
(down shift)
go off duty [work]

783. xià bù liǎo tái
下 不 了 台
(down not the stage)
to feel embarrassed

784. xiā chě dàn
瞎 扯 蛋
(blind pull egg)
to make up; fabricate

785. xiā hùn
瞎 混
(blind mix)
to loaf about

786. xià jiǔ de cài
下 酒 的 菜
(down wine food)
food that goes with wine

787. xià liú
下 流
(down flow)
said of someone who uses profane language and has his
    mind in the gutter; a "dirty old man"

788. xiā shuō
瞎 说
(blind talk)
talks rubbish irresponsibly

111

789. **xià xiāng**
下 乡
(down country)
to go to the country side

790. **xiān shàng chē hòu bǔ piào**
先 上 车 後 补 票
(get on bus first, later buy ticket)
get pregnant first, then get married

791. **xiǎng bú dào**
想 不 到
(think not reach)
not to expect; unexpected

792. **xiǎng bù qǐ lái**
想 不 起 来
(think not get up)
unable to recall

793. **xiǎng fāng (bàn) fǎ**
想 方 (办) 法
(think method)
do everything possible; try every means by hook or crook

794. **xiāng jiāo**
香 蕉
(banana)
a Chinese person who grew up in the U.S. (yellow
　　　outside, white inside) (humorously)

795. **xiǎng lái xiǎng qù**
想 来 想 去
(think come think go)
to rack one's brain

796. **xiǎo biàn**
小 便
(minor convenience)
to urinate

797. **xiǎo bù diǎn**
小 不 点
(small not dot)
a very small person

798. **xiǎo de**
晓 得
(morning get)
to know

799. **xiǎo ér kē**
小 儿 科
(small son (pediatrics) department)
to be stingy

800. **xiǎo fèi**
小 费
(small spend)
tip

801. **xiǎo hào**
小 号
(small number)
to urinate (Taiwan)

802. **xiào huà**
笑 话
(laugh speech)
joke

803. **xiáo huǒ zi**
小 伙 子
(small fellow)
a guy; young man

804. **xiáo lǎo pó**
小 老 婆
(small wife)
concubine

113

805. xiǎo mèi
小 妹
(little sister)
a young waitress; younger sister

806. xiào miàn hǔ
笑 面 虎
(laugh face tiger)
a wicked person; a bad guy with a smiling face

807. xiǎo qì guǐ
小 气 鬼
(small air devil)
a stingy person; a miser

808. xiǎo shuō
小 说
(small talk)
novel (book)

809. xiǎo wū jiàn dà wū
小 巫 见 大 巫
(small witch see big witch)
to be insignificant by comparison; can not compare with

810. xiǎo xīn
小 心
(small heart)
be careful!; take care!

811. xiǎo xīn yì yì
小 心 翼 翼
(careful wings)
to be extremely careful

812. xiǎo yì sī
小 意 思
(small meaning)
token (of appreciation)

813.   xiě bái zì
写 白 字
(write white character)
write wrong character

814.   xīn dǎn jù liè
心 胆 俱 裂
(heart gall both broke)
to be frightened out of one's wits; to quake in one's boots

815.   xīn gān bǎo bèi
心 肝 宝 贝
(heart liver treasure)
a doting mother may refer to her son as such

816.   xīn huáng yì luàn
心 慌 意 乱
(heart aggitated mind mess)
confused

817.   xīn jīng dǎn zhàn
心 惊 胆 颤
(heart afraid gall bladder afraid)
to tremble with fear

818.   xìn kǒu kāi hé
信 口 开 河
(letter mouth open river) \
to say whatever comes to mind; talks at random; nonsense;
                                          talks irresponsibly

819.   xīn kǒu rú yī
心 口 如 一
(heart mouth as if one)
to say what one thinks; to speak one's mind

820.   xīn kuān liàng dà
心 宽 量 大
(heart wide capacity big)
big hearted; generous; considerate

821. xīn mǎn yì zú
心 满 意 足
(heart full easy sufficient)
completly satisfied; content with

822. xīn shén bú dìng
心 神 不 定
(heart mind not steady)
to have no peace of mind; be ill at ease; restless; uneasy

823. xīn wú èr yòng
心 无 二 用
(heart not two use)
can't do two things at the same time

824. xīn xīn kǔ kǔ
辛 辛 苦 苦
(hard hard bitter bitter)
arduously; take great pains; very difficult; strenuous

825. xīn zhí kǒu kuài
心 直 口 快
(heart straight mouth quick)
to be outspoken; straightforward, say what one thinks
                                    without hesitation

826. xīng fēng zuò làng
兴 风 作 浪
(make wind make waves)
stir up trouble; "make waves"

827. xìng qù
兴 趣
(feelings interest)
an interest in (something)

828. xíng xíng sè sè
形 形 色 色
(shape color)
of every shape and hue; of every description; of many
                kinds and varieties; various

829. **xíng yǐng bù lí**
形 影 不 离
(shape shadow not separated)
(two people) inseparable

830. **xiù hua zhěn tóu**
绣 花 枕 头
(flower embroidered pillow)
a person who is beautiful on the outside but straw on the inside (worthless)

831. **xǔ xǔ duō duō**
许 许 多 多
(about many)
a great number of; many; a lot of; plenty of

832. **xū yǒu qí biǎo**
虚 有 其 表
(unreal have his superficial)
handsome but lacking substance, ability, or virility

833. **xué ér bú yàn**
学 而 不 厌
(learn and not dislike)
never tire of learning

834. **xuě shàng jiā shuāng**
雪 上 加 霜
(snow top add frost)
one disaster after another

835. **xuē zú shì lǚ**
削 足 适 履
(cut feet fit shoe)
force evidence to fit the theory; do not stick to one's principle; force oneself to adapt to a situation

Y

836.   **yǎ kǒu wú yán**
哑 口 无 言
(dumb mouth nothing speak)
to render speechless

837.   **yā wān le yāo**
压 弯 了 腰
(press bend waist)
to be bent with a heavy burden

838.   **yā zi sǐ le zuǐ hái yìng**
鸭 子 死 了 嘴 还 硬
(duck died mouth still hard)
to be too stuborn to admit mistakes

839.   **yǎn gāo shǒu dī**
眼 高 手 低
(eye high hand low)
one who has high aspirations but low ability

840.   **yǎn guān liù lù**
眼 观 六 路
(eyes see 6 roads)
to keep an eye on everything

841.   **yǎn guān sì fāng**
眼 观 四 方
(eyes see 4 directions)
to keep an eye on everything

842. **yǎn guāng duǎn qiǎn**
眼 光 短 浅
(eye bright too shallow)
one who is satisfied with small profits; short sighted; does
not see the big picture for the future

843. **yán guò qí shí**
言 过 其 实
(speaks over truth)
stretch the truth; draw the long bow; exaggerate

844. **yǎn hóng**
眼 红
(eye red)
green with envy

845. **yǎn jīng chī bīng qí lín**
眼 睛 吃 冰 淇 淋
(eye eat ice cream)
look but not touch pretty girls

846. **yáng guǐ zi**
洋 鬼 子
(ocean devil)
"foreign devil" (any westerner)

847. **yáng yáng dà guān**
洋 洋 大 观
(abundant...big view)
spectacular

848. **yào bù rán**
要 不 然
(want not yet)
otherwise; if not

849. **yào bú shì**
要 不 是
(want not yes)
if not

119

850. yáo lái yáo qù
      摇 来 摇 去
      (shake come shake go)
      to rock back and forth

851. yào nǐ hǎo kàn
      要 你 好 看
      (want you good look)
      to not show due respect to someone; to get even with
                                              someone

852. yào xiǎo xīn
      要 小 心
      (should small heart)
      must take great care; watch one's step; be cautious

853. yáo yáo lǐng xiān
      遥 遥 领 先
      (far away far away collar first)
      to be way ahead; have a good lead

854. yáo yáo yù zhuì
      摇 摇 欲 坠
      (shake going to fall)
      be about to fall apart; rickety; instable

855. yě bù yí dìng
      也 不 一 定
      (also not for sure)
      maybe or maybe not

856. yě jiù shì shuō
      也 就 是 说
      (also then is speak)
      that is to say; it also means

857. yé xǔ
      也 许
      (also permit)
      perhaps, maybe

858.   yí bù yí bù (de)
一　步　一　步（的）
(one step one step)
step by step

859.   yì diǎn xiǎo shì
一　点　小　事
(one dot small thing)
it's nothing

860.   yì diǎn yě bù
一　点　也　不
(a little also not)
not at all...

861.   yì diǎn zhé yě méi yǒu
一　点　辙　也　没　有
(a little method also nothing)
nothing can be done about it

862.   yí dù zi cǎo
一　肚　子　草
(stomach of grass)
someone who has no ability

863.   yī fān fēng shùn
一　帆　风　顺
(a sail wind smooth)
have a smooth trip; smooth sailing

864.   yí gè bàn ----
一　个　半　-----
(one half ----)
one and one half ----

865.   yí ge bí kǒng chū qì
一　个　鼻　孔　出　气
(breathe through the same nostril)
"sing out of the same songbook"; to be in complete
         agreement

121

866. yí gè jìn
      一 个 劲
      (one spirit)
      to keep on doing something

867. yì guō zhōu
      一 锅 粥
      (a pot of gruel)
      a complete mess

868. yí hàn
      遗 憾
      (loss sorry)
      to be sorry

869. yì huǐ jiàn
      一 会 见
      (one moment see)
      see you later (in a bit)

870. yì kǒu qì
      一 口 气
      (one mouth breath)
      in one breath

871. yì lái
      一 来
      (one come)
      in the first place; on the one hand

872. yí lù duō bǎo zhòng
      一 路 多 保 重
      (one way more take care)
      take care of yourself on the trip

873. yí lù huò
      一 路 货
      (one road merchandise)
      of the same kind; birds of a feather

874. **yí lù píng ān**
一 路 平 安
(journey peaceful peaceful)
to have a safe and peaceful journey; Bon Voyage!

875. **yí lù shùn fēng**
一 路 顺 风
(on the way smooth wind)
have a good trip

876. **yì máo bù bá**
一 毛 不 拔
(one hair not pulled out)
someone who wouldn't even give one hair; a stingy
        person; a "tight wad"

877. **yì mó yí yàng**
一 模 一 样
(one model one form)
exactly alike

878. **yì qīng èr chǔ**
一 清 二 楚
(one clear two clear)
perfectly clear

879. **yí qù bú fù fǎn**
一 去 不 复 返
(one go not come back)
gone forever; never to return

880. **yì rú fǎn zhǎng**
易 如 反 掌
(easy as turn over (one's) palm)
very easy to do

881. **yì shǒu zhē tiān**
一 手 遮 天
(one hand cover sky)
to fool the people

882.　yì tiān dào wǎn
　　　一　天　到　晚
　　　(one day reach night)
　　　all the live long day; from dawn to dusk

883.　yí wàng wú jì
　　　一　望　无　际
　　　(look for no bound)
　　　limitless; as far as the eye can see

884.　yì xīn yí yì
　　　一　心　一　意
　　　(one heart one idea)
　　　with great determination

885.　yì yán nán jìn
　　　一　言　难　尽
　　　(one remark difficult end)
　　　it's a long story

886.　yì yán wéi dìng
　　　一　言　为　定
　　　(one word make decision)
　　　That's settled then; it's a date.

887.　yí yàng yí gè
　　　一　样　一　个
　　　(one kind one)
　　　one of each

888.　yì zhí
　　　一　直
　　　(one straight)
　　　all along; all the while; straight on; so far

889.　yī zhī bàn jiě
　　　一　知　半　解
　　　(one know half understand)
　　　half-baked knowledge

890. yòng bù zháo
用 不 着
(use not reach)
don't need

891. yòng gōng
用 功
(use merit)
diligently; work hard

892. yǒng yuǎn
永 远
(eternal far)
always; forever

893. yóu bù dé
由 不 得
(reason not)
involuntarily; unable to do as one pleases; cannot help

894. yǒu diǎn
有 点
(have dot)
somewhat; a bit

895. yǒu guān xi
有 关 系
(to have connections)
to have friends or relations in high places who can help
                                                                one succeed

896. yóu hú lú
油 葫 芦
(field cricket)
to be fat; plump; chubby

897. yǒu kě néng
有 可 能
(can do)
to be possible; that's possible

898.　yǒu kòng
有　空
(have empty)
to be free; have spare time

899.　yǒu lì yǒu bì
有　利　有　弊
(have advantage have disadvantage)
have advantages and disadvantages

900.　yǒu máo bìng
有　毛　病
(have fur sick)
to be sick; have something malfunction; it doesn't work

901.　yǒu mén lù
有　门　路
(to have door road)
to know the ropes; to be on the right track; resourceful

902.　yǒu shén me shì
有　什　么　事
(have what thing?)
What's the matter?

903.　yǒu shēng qì
有　生　气
(have animate energy)
dynamic; full of vitality

904.　yǒu shí (hòu)
有　时　(候)
(have time)
once in a while, sometimes

905.　yǒu shuǐ píng
有　水　平
(have water standard)
to be up to a certain standard

906.   **yǒu tiáo yǒu lǐ**
有 条 有 理
(have strip have reason)
methodically; systematically

907.   **yǒu xǐ**
有 喜
(have happines)
to be pregnant

908.   **yǒu yàng xué yàng**
有 样 学 样
(have kind learn kind)
to mimick someone; to do as another does

909.   **yǒu yì shūo yī, yǒu èr shūo èr**
有 一 说 一 有 二 说 二
(have one say one, have two say two)
to call a spade a spade

910.   **yǒu yì si**
有 意 思
(have meaning)
interesting; significant; meaningful

911.   **yóu yǒng**
游 泳
(swim)
to play Mahjong; to swim

912.   **yǔ zhòng bù tóng**
与 众 不 同
(with everyone not same)
out of the ordinary

913.   **yǔ zhòu fēi xíng yuán (tài kōng rén)**
宇 宙 飞 行 员 (太 空 人)
(universe fly go person)
astronaut

914. yuán lái
      原 来
      (origin come)
      originally, actually

915. yuán lái rú cǐ
      原 来 如 此
      (originally like this)
      is that so!

916. yuán liàng
      原 谅
      (original sorry)
      to apologize; to excuse; forgive

917. yuán zǐ néng
      原 子 能
      (atomic able)
      atomic energy

918. yùe laí yùe (X)   [an adverb or expression (X) follows]
      越 来 越 (X)
      (over come over)
      more and more (X); even more (X)

919. **zá qī zá bā**
杂 七 杂 八
(mix 7's mix 8's)
lots of things

920. **zài bǎi máng zhōng**
在 百 忙 中
(at 100 busy among)
in the middle of busy affairs

921. **zài bù rán...**
再 不 然
(again not so)
otherwise

922. **zài háo yě méi yǒu le!**
再 好 也 没 有 了
(again good also not have)
it couldn't be better

923. **zài huì**
再 会
(again meet)
goodbye; until we meet again; see you later

924. **zài jiàn**
再 见
(again see)
goodbye; until we meet again; see you later

925. zài lái yí ge
再 来 一 个
(again come one)
encore

926. zǎo ān
早 安
(early peace)
good morning

927. zāo gāo
糟 糕
(messy cake)
expression of disgust at something; holy cow!; what a
pity! Oh, Oh!

928. zāo le
糟 了
(mess)
Oh heck; damn!

929. zěn me bàn?
怎 么 办
(what to do)
what can be done about it ?

930. zén me gǎo de
怎 么 搞 的
(how come do)
how it comes to such a mess? (said to someone who
annoys you)

931. zěn me le?
怎 么 了
(how)
what happened?; how is it?; what's wrong?

932. zěn me yàng
怎 么 样
(how kind)
how are things? what do you think? so what? what's up?

933. **zěn me yǐ huí shì**
怎 么 一 回 事
(how one matter)
what's it all about? what's going on? what's this?

934. **zěn me zhè me?**
怎 么 这 么 ---- (+ your phrase)
(how is this ----)
how is it that ----?; why ----?; how come ----?

935. **zěn me zhèn me zāo gāo!**
怎 么 这 么 糟 糕
(how come it is such a mess)
how come this happened!

936. **zén me zǒu?**
怎 么 走
(how to go?)
how to get to?

937. **zhǎng de (hǎo) tián**
长 得 （好） 甜
(develop sweet)
said of sweet girls; to look sweet (esp. with dimples)

938. **zhāng sān lǐ sì**
张 三 李 四
(Zhang 3. Li 4)
John Doe; Mary Brown (any person)

939. **zhǎng shàng míng zhū**
掌 上 明 珠
(palm top bright pearl)
"a pearl on the palm"; a parent refers affectionately to a
       beloved daughter

940. **zhǎng wāi le xīn yǎn**
长 歪 了 心 眼
(grow crooked heart eye)
evil; unkind; wicked

941. zhǎo dì fāng liáng kuài
找 地 方 凉 快
(find a place to cool off)
it's none of your business; go away

942. zhào liào
照 料
(take material)
to look after

943. zhǎo mǎ zi
找 马 子
(look for horse)
to "pick up" a girl (in a bar, etc.) (Taiwan)

944. zhāo Qín mù Chǔ
朝 秦 暮 楚
(serving Qin in the morning and Chu in the evening)
quick to switch sides

945. zhǎo shēng huó
找 生 活
(find life)
to earn a living

946. zhǎo sǐ a
找 死 啊
(look for death)
"asking for trouble"; "spoiling for a fight"

947. zhè rén hěn yóu
这 人 很 油
(this person very oily)
one who is "slippery" and makes promises one does not
keep

948. zhēn bù qiǎo
真 不 巧
(really not opportune)
unfortunately

949. **zhēn de shì**
真 的 是
(real is)
well really! the idea!

950. **zhēn yí hàn**
真 遗 憾
(really sorry)
what a pity!

951. **zhēn zāo gāo**
真 糟 糕
(really a mess)
it's really too bad

952. **zhèng hǎo**
正 好
(just good)
just at the right time; by coincidence

953. **zhèng shì**
正 是
(exact is)
that is it exactly; the very thing

954. **zhèng yào**
正 要
(straight want)
just going to

955. **zhǐ hǎo**
只 好
(only good)
to accept reluctantly something other than one's first
choice

956. **zhǐ jī mà gǒu**
指 鸡 骂 狗
(point to chicken scold dog)
to scold someone other than the real culprit in order to
teach a lesson

957. zhǐ lù wéi mǎ
指 鹿 为 马
(point deer for horse)
to be mistaken

958. zhí qù
知 趣
(know interesting)
to be tactful

959. zhì ruò wǎng wén
置 若 罔 闻
(put as if no hear)
turn a deaf ear to; pay no attention to

960. zhǐ sāng mà huái
指 桑 骂 槐
(point at the mulberry and scold the locust)
to scold someone other than the real culprit in order to
teach a lesson

961. zhí shǒu huà jiǎo
指 手 画 脚
(point hand picture foot)
to gesture with hands while speaking

962. zhòng yào
重 要
(heavy want)
important

963. zhōu dào
周 到
(complete arrive)
to be considerate; thoughtful

964. zhǔ chí
主 持
(chief control)
direct; manage; be in charge of

965. zhú gān
竹 竿
(bamboo stick)
a tall skinny person; a "bean pole"

966. zhù kǒu
住 口
(stop mouth)
shut up!

967. zhù yì
注 意
(note idea)
pay attention to

968. zhuā biàn zi
抓 辫 子
(sieze one's hair braid)
to seize on one's mistake or failure

969. zhuā ěr náo sāi
抓 耳 挠 腮
(scratch ear scratch cheek)
to be at a loss as to what to do or say

970. zhuǎn dá
转 达
(pass reach)
to convey; communicate

971. zhuǎn gào
转 告
(turn around tell)
pass on the message

972. zhuàn lái zhuàn qù
转 来 转 去
(turn come turn go)
mill around

973. zhuān xīn
专 心
(attentive heart)
to pay attention; concentrate on something

974. zhuǎn yǎn
转 眼
(turn eye)
in the twinkling of an eye; fast; in a quick moment

975. zhuàn zhuàn
转 转
(to turn around)
to go out

976. zhuō jīn jiàn zhǒu
捉 襟 见 肘
(fasten coat collar see elbow)
to have more problems that one can handle; not able to
cope with

977. zì bái
自 白
(self white)
to confess; to "make a clean breast of it"

978. zì lā zì chàng
自 拉 自 唱
(oneself play instrument oneself sing)
to praise oneself; "to blow one's own horn"

979. zì jǐ dǎ zì jǐ de zuǐ ba
自 己 打 自 己 的 嘴 巴
(to hit one's own mouth)
to contradict one's self

980. zì jǐ laí
自 己 来
(oneself come)
the help oneself

136

981. zì qī qī rén
自 欺 欺 人
(self cheat cheat people)
deceive yourself as well as others

982. zì shǐ zhì zhōng
自 始 至 终
(from beginning to end)
all the time

983. zì wǒ jiè shào yí xià
自 我 介 绍 一 下
(self I introduce)
to introduce oneself

984. zì yóu huó dòng
自 由 活 动
(free life move)
go about by oneself; need not stay with a group; to be "on
                                                    your own"

985. zǒng ér yán zhī
总 而 言 之
(result speak of)
in sum; after all is said and done; in the final analysis

986. zǒu ba!
走 吧 !
(go!)
let's go!

987. zóu gǒu
走 狗
(running dog)
a lacky

988. zóu hǎo
走 好
(walk good)
good bye! take care!

989.   zóu hòu mén
       走 後 门
       (go rear door)
       to make back door deals

990.   zǒu kāi
       走 开
       (go open)
       go away!; get out of the way!

991.   zǒu le yǎn
       走 了 眼
       (go eye)
       to judge incorrectly

992.   zǒu lù
       走 路
       (go road)
       walk

993.   zǒu lù bù zhǎng yǎn jīng
       走 路 不 长 眼 睛
       (go walk not grow eye)
       to not watch where one is walking

994.   zǒu mǎ kàn huā
       走 马 看 花
       (go by horse look flowers)
       to go over things quickly; scratch the surface; take a brief
                                                      look at

995.   zǒu yí bù shì yí bù
       走 一 步 是 一 步
       (go one step is one step)
       do as you see fit; do as much as you can

996.   zǒu yì zǒu
       走 一 走
       (walk walk)
       just walk around

997. zuān niú jiǎo jiān
钻 牛 角 尖
(penetrate points of cow horns)
to think too deeply about a problem with a simple solution

998. zuǐ zhēn tián
嘴 真 甜
(mouth really sweet)
to be a flatterer; one who sweet talks

999. zuò guài
作 怪
(be strange)
to be a nuisance; "a pain in the neck"

1000. zuò lěng bǎn dèng
坐 冷 板 凳
(sit on a cold wood stool)
to be given the cold shoulder

1001. zuò niú zuò mǎ
作 牛 作 马
(be ox be horse)
to live like a beast of burden

1002. zuǒ yòu
左 右
(left right)
about; both sides; approximately

1003. zuǒ yòu shǒu
左 右 手
(left right hand)
to be a good helper; a "right hand man"

Appendix A .....

Bibliography

1. Ann, T.K. (1982). *Cracking the Chinese Puzzles*, Vol. 1- 5. Hong Kong. Stockflows Co., Ltd.
2. Barron's Educational Series. *201 Chinese Verbs - Compounds and Phrases for Everyday Use.*
3. Beijing Language Institute (1984). *Spoken Chinese 900.* Beijing, China.
4._____ (1985). *A Reverse Chinese-English Dictionary.* Beijing, China. Commercial Press.
5. _____ (1990). *Conversational Chinese 301.* Beijing, China.
6. Chang, Raymond and Margaret Chang (1983). *Speaking of Chinese.* New York and London. W.W. Norton & Co.
7. Chao, Ren Yuen (1958). *A Grammar of Spoken Chinese.* University of California Press.
8. Chen, Ru (1991). *Chinese Situational Dialogues.* Peking University Press.
9. Chen, Ta-Tuan, *et. al.* (1989a). *Chinese Primer - Lessons.* Cambridge, Mass., and London, England. Harvard University Press.
10. _____ (1989b). *Chinese Primer - Notes & Exercises.* Cambridge, Mass., and London, England. Harvard University Press.
11. Chen, Zhiyuan, Editor (1981). *A Chinese / English Handbook of Idioms.* Hong Kong. Joint Publishing Co.
12. Chew, Chauncey C. (1983). *A Reference Grammar of Mandarin Chinese for Speakers of English.* Peter Lang, Publisher.
13. *Chinese for Beginners* (1976). Peking University. Foreign Language Press.
14. *Chinese 300.* (1984). Beijing, China. Chinese Language Library/Sinolingua.
15. Ching, Eugene and Nora Ching (1977). *201 Chinese Verbs - Compounds and Phrases for Everyday Use.* Barron's Educational Series, Inc.
16. Chou, Chih-Ping and Der-Lin Chao (1992). *Intermediate Reader of Modern Chinese.* Princeton University Press.
17. Cloy, Rita Mei-Wah (1989). *Understanding Chinese - A Guide to the Usage of Chinese Characters.* San Francisco, Calif. China West Books.

140

18. *Concise Chinese-English Dictionary* (1981). Singapore. World Book Company
19. Daniel, Ray (1993). *Making Out in Chinese.* Charles E. Tuttle Co.
20. De Mente, Boye Lafayette (1996). *NTC's Dictionary of China's Cultural Code Words.* Lincolnwood, Ill. NTC Publishing Group.
21. DeFrancis, John (1963). *Beginning Chinese.* New Haven and London. Yale University Press.
22. _____ (1964). *Intermediate Chinese.* Yale Linguistic Series. New Haven and London. Yale University Press.
23. *Dictionary of Spoken Chinese* (1968). Yale University, Conn. Institute of Far Eastern Languages.
24. Dillon, Kaining, and Sanders (1990). *Essential Chinese (Mandarin).* Penguin Books.
25. Du, Rong and Helen T. Lin, (1985). *Speaking Chinese About China.* Beijing, China. Sinolingua.
26. Faculty of Beijing Language Institute (1981). *New Chinese 300 - A Beginning Language Course.* Boston, Mass. Cheng & Tsui Co.
27. Faculty of Peking University (1971). *Modern Chinese - A Basic Course.* New York. Dover Publications, Inc.
28. _____ (1981). *Modern Chinese - A Second Course.* New York. Dover Publications, Inc.
29. Feng, Naikang and Songgin Li (1987). *A Handbook of Chinese-English Conversations for Tourists.* Tourism Education Press.
30. Heng, Xiao-Jun and Xue Zhi Zhang (1988). *A Chinese / English Dictionary of Idioms and Proverbs.* Tübingen, Germany. Max Niemeyer, Pub.
31. Hong, Beverly (1991). *Speak Chinese Today - A Basic Course In The Modern Language.* Charles E. Tuttle Co.
32. Hu, Jerome P. and Stephen C. Lee (1992). *Basic Chinese Vocabulary.* Lincolnwood, Ill. Passport Books, NTC Publishing Group.
33. Huang, Zheng Cheng *et. al.* (1986). *Chinese for Today.* Beijing Language Institute. San Francisco, Calif. China Books and Periodicals.
34. Jin, Shao Zhi (1988). *An Introduction to Modern Chinese Vocabulary.* Beijing, China. Sinolingua.
35. Kan, Qian (1995). *Colloquial Chinese - A Complete Language Course.* London. Routledge
36. *Learners' Chinese/English Dictionary* (1979). The Shanghai Book Co.
37. Li, Charles N. and Sandra A. Thompson (1981). *Mandarin Chinese - A Functional Reference Grammar.* University of California Press.
38. *Listening and Speaking - Intermediate Chinese* (1990). Beijing, China. Beijing Language Institute Press.

39. Lu, John H. T. (1987). *Mandarin Chinese*, Vol. 1. Tallahassee, Fla. East Oak House Publishing Co.
40. Ming, Liu and King Chen Hsing-yeh (1984). *Basic Chinese*. Hong Kong. Chinese University of Hong Kong.
41. Mok, Ellie Mao (1975). *Chinese for Beginners*. New York. Fredrick Ungar Publishing Co.
42. *Modern Chinese - Beginners Course* (1986). Beijing, China. Beijing Language Institute Prèss/Sinolingua.
43. Montanaro, John (1981). *Chinese / English Phrase Book for Travelers*. Yale University, Conn. John Wiley & Sons.
44. Ning, Cynthia (1993). *Communicating in Chinese*. Yale University, Conn. Far Eastern Publication
45. Pao, Donald (1968). *Practical Chinese Conversation*. Taiwan. Cave Books Ltd.
46. Peng, Tan-Huay (1987). *Chinese Idioms*. Singapore. Time Books International.
47. *Practical Chinese* (1990). Taipei, Republic of China. Wen Shang Publisher.
48. Sanders, Irene (1986). *The Right Word in Chinese*. Hong Kong. The Commercial Press Ltd.
49. Scurfield, Elizabeth (1992). *Chinese - A Complete Course for Beginners*. NTC publishing Group.
50. Sinolingua (1980c). *Elementary Chinese Readers*. Books 1- 5. Beijing, China.
51. _____ (1990a). *Spoken Chinese*. Beijing, China.
52. _____ (1990b). *"Hello" - Practical Dialogues for Home, School, Social Life, and Travel*. Beijing, China. Chinese Intern'l Book Trading Corp
53. _____ (1991). *Communicative Chinese*. Beijing, China.
54. Season, Samuel M. Wong (1975). *Chinese Idioms and Phrases*. Commercial Press.
55. Tan, Situ (1984). *Best Chinese Idioms*. Hong Kong. Hai Feng Publishing Co.
56. _____, Tang Bowen, and Ding Cong (1988). *Best Chinese Idioms,* Vol. 2. Hong Kong. Hai Feng Publishing Co
57. Tung, P.C. and D.E. Pollard (1982). *Colloquial Chinese*. London and New York. Routledge
58. Tung, Wendy (1991). *Easy Chinese - Phrasebook & Dictionary*. Lincolnwood, Ill. Passport Books, NTC Publishing Group
59. Wang, Ding-Ho (1981). *Chinese Slang*. Taipei, Republic of China. Dunhuang Shuju. (Based on the Chinese vocabulary of the Yale textbook *Chinese Dialogs*.)

60. Wang, Guozhang (1992). *Practical Spoken Chinese*. Beijing, China. Peoples University of China
61. Wang, James J. (1994). *Outrageous Chinese*. San Francisco, Calif. China Book & Periodicals.
62. Wang, Peggy (1986). *Language in Chinese*. Montreal, Canada. SODILIS, Editeur Libraire.
63. Wang, Xiaopen and Qiangong Liu (1993). *Chinese-English Communication in Chinese*. Peking University P
64. Wu, Zhaoyi *et. al.* (1983). *The English-Chinese Pinyin Pocket Dictionary*. Beijing, China. New World Press.
65. Yee, Ching and John Smithback (1991). *Fun With Chinese Idioms* , Vol I. Singapore. Federal Publications.
66. Zeng, Zifan (1986). *Colloquial Cantonese and Putonghua Equivalents*. Hong Kong. Joint Publishing Co
67. Zhong, Qin (1980). *Chinese For You - Learn to Speak Putonghua*. Hong Kong. Man Hai Language Publication
68. _____ (1985). *Everyday Chinese - Selected Prose Readings*. Beijing, China. New World Press.
69. Zhou, Yimin and James J. Wang (1995). *Mutant Mandarin - A guide to New Chinese Slang*. San Francisco, Calif. China Book and Periodical

Appendix B .....

English Code Word Index
to Chinese Expression Numbers in the Dictionary

A

abandon
    something
    472
ability 127, 862
able to cope 553
about 193
abundant 55
accompany one
    66
acrobat 505
act crazy 637,
    668
act dumb 185
activity 342
actually 600
afraid 275, 439,
    580, 581
agitated 599
agreement 865
aimlessly 602
all around 699
all directions 224
all embracing 42
all kinds of
    things 286
all night long
    736
all split up 698
all the same 29
all the time 982

all the while 888
all thumbs 53
almost 128
always 892
always win 26
amazed 146
amazing 474
amenable 152
amorous 261
angry 223, 658
angry person 363
anxious 751
apologize 916
appear crazy -27
arduously 824
as expected 76
as you wish 703
ashamed to ask
    74
ask advice 616
assure you 41
astronaut 713,
    913
at a loss 969
at least 598
at wit's end 646
atomic energy
    917
attractive 590

B

baby sitter 43
bad check 419
bad guy 352
banana 794
bare necessities
    68
bargain 389
bark is bigger
    467
be good at 557
be happy 422
be popular 6
bear hardship 147
begin doing 228
beginner 125
behave yourself
    65
beloved daughter
    939
bent with burden
    837
besides 481
best 221
better than
    nothing 476
beyond
    recognition
    628
bicycle 729
big nose 277

Code Word Index

Code Word Index

doting mother 815

drinking spree 506

drop dead 267

dumb mistake 566

dynamic 903

E

earn living 945

easy to do 880

eat 141

eat or not 1

egg head 17

embarrass 130, 540

embarrassed 95, 783

encore 925

endless stream 492

enjoy 312

enough! enough! 323

enthuastic 538, 627

etc. 212

every corner 770

everyone 284, 631

evil 940

evil intentions 520

exactly alike 877

exaggerate 379, 843

excuse me 398, 400, 461, 493, 611

exhausted 36

extremely 253

extremely good 320

F

fabricate 784

fact 669

fail 343, 710

fail exam 8

fair 288

fall 208

fall behind 750

fall in love 3

family 376

famous 333, 661, 707

fast 974

fatso 319

fed up 574

feel at home 706

few words 641

final analysis 302, 985

find fault 396

find time 160, 161

first place 871

fixed price 87

flamboyant 485

flat chested 254

flatter 308, 582

flatterer 998

flirt 144, 587

food 786

food awful 560

- fool 164

fool the people 881

foolish looking 644

for example 57

for sure 438

force evidence 835

foreign devil 846-

forget it 447, 702

forgive me 613

formalities 33

G

fortunately 327

frank 533

frightened 814

fruitless trip 18

frustrated 755

full of life 659

game is over 747

gangster 331

general idea 192

generous 820

geomancy 262

gesture 961

get lost 304, 306

get out 102, 621

get to 936

getting late 121

girl flirt 256

give regards 761

give up 35, 187, 249

glib 189

go "all out" 527

go away 941, 990

go dutch 281

go out 975

go shopping 650

go too far 114

go with crowd 704

God knows! 724

gone forever 879

good for nothing 138, 155

good guy 10

good lead 853

Good Lord! 722

good morning 926

good trip 875

good-bye 258, 278, 923, 924

goose bumps 372

Code Word Index

Code Word Index

limitless 883
listening 242
literate 633
live 150, 597
live like a beast
    1001
loaf about 785
long story 885
long time 34
long way to go
    313
long winded 536
look after 942
look all around
    752
look around 426
look sweet 937
lose face 45
lose job 5
lose temper 672
losing end 149
lot of stuff 478
lots of things 919
lucky hit 742

M

macho 186
make deals 989
make fun 746
make trouble 368
make waves 826
malfunction 900
manage 964
many 831
married 22, 135
married life 264
maybe 855
mean person 332,
    455
mean to say 561
mediocre 93
meet again 336
mess 867, 930
midnight oil 725

might as well 88
mill around 972
mimic 908
mischief 454
miser 728
mistaken 957
mistreat 171
moment's notice
    480
money 401, 593,
    614
monk 166
more and more
    918
moreover 240
my goodness
    321

N

nag 578
natural tragedy
    245
naughty 726
never before 440
never give up 82
never mind 71,
    524, 529
never satisfied
    719
no alternative 526
no choice 83, 252
no competition
    143
no free lunch 535
no hope 745
no matter what
    91, 92
no more than 112
no need 119
no see 322
no wonder 296
noisy 565
non stop talker
    615

nonsense 362,
    382, 534, 818
not as bad 123
not at all 860
not bad 77
not bear to see
    126
not deserve 90
not feel well 110
not figure out 19
not only 79
not perfect 109
not sure 767
not touch girls
    845
not understand
    503
not watch 993
not worth doing
    244
nothing special
    122
novel 808
nuisance 999

O

obvious 545
occupations 601
odds and ends
    371, 479
off and on 233
off duty 782
offer dinner 397
old hand 463
old maid 459
old partner 456
on edge 369
on guard 158
on the way 690
on your own 984
one and only 416
one of each 887
one's own way
    705

148

Code Word Index

Code Word Index

Code Word Index

tens of thousands 134

terror stricken 202

text 436

that is to say 856

that's all 413

that's enough 211

that's great 555, 558, 711

that's OK 70

that's right 673

the boss 457

theory 469

think 570

think deeply 997

tiger tail 596

tight wad 876

time comes 207

time marches on 294

tip 800

tired of hearing 20

tired of seeing 15

to bargain 718

to care 299

to chat 717

to confess 978

to cry 444

to doze 390

to flirt 501

to jog 514

to judge 991

to know 475

to reveal 399

token 812

tongue twister 622

too bad 715, 951

total confusion 619

touchy 588

tremble 817

trouble 257, 311, 721, 946

true or false 660

trust to luck 732

truth 433

turn deaf ear 959

turn pale 716

two faced 375

ZI

ugly 562

ulterior motives 69

unchaste 594, 595

undecided 415

understand 543

unearned 387

unexpected 791

unexpectedly 530

unfortunately 948

unlucky 206

unpopular 85, 140

unrealistic 696

unwillingly 449

up a tree 453

urgent 670

urinate 402, 651, 796, 801

use one's head 225

used to 781

V

vacation 247

vain compliments 777

various 828

very good 220, 730

very happy 780

very nice 572

very poor 328, 665

very thing 953

vigor 341

vigor and vitality 656

W

walk 992

walk around 301, 996

waste breath 12

waste effort 11, 24

waste life 577

watch one's step 852

we're finished 744

well really 949

went wrong 169

wet dream 585

what a pity 927, 950

what country? 571

what happened? 674, 931

what then? 338

what to do? 273, 928

what's done is done 657

what's going on? 933

what's the matter? 902

what's the rush? 519

what's up? 612, 655, 932

what's wrong? 575

whisper 393

Code Word Index

white wash 46
who says so? 554
wicked 806
wife 153
wife unfaithful
   196
window shopping
   300
without
   hesitation 100
wonderful 473
work 648

work hard 891
workaholic 291
worry 201
worthless 830
wrong character
   813
wrong crowd 489
wrong idea 7

Y

yellow race 357

you're fired 610
you're right 522
you're welcome
   103, 115
young man 803
young waitress
   805
your turn 265
you're welcome
   64